SIX FIGURES

Mixing Friendship & Business
... Like a Good Martini

D1563429

Barbara Parsons

Lauri Mitchell

Lee Knapp

Susan Cullen

Gina McAndrew

Nicolle Carfagnini

Six Figures

Mixing Friendship and Business
... Like a Good Martini

By Barbara Parsons, Lauri Mitchell, Lee Knapp,
Susan Cullen, Gina McAndrew, Nicolle Carfagnini

Six Figures Publishing

www.SixFiguresBook.com
Copyright © 2012
All rights reserved.

Library of Congress Control Number: 2012906803
ISBN: 978-0-9837393-0-2

Cover and Interior Design:
Jack & Cathy Davis, www.DavisCreative.com

Epigraph quote by permission — Bernie DeKoven
www.DeepFun.com

DEDICATION

We dedicate our story to women
who have faced life's most difficult
challenges head on, sometimes with
only their girlfriends to lean on.

Together, we help each other forge
ahead in search of something better.

4/8/14

Gina McAndren

Barbara Parsons

Lauri Mitchell

"When the fun gets deep enough,
it can heal the world."
— Bernie DeKoven

CONTENTS

Girls perform "Bad Girls" at business conference talent show.

ONE

Who We Are Depends on the Story We Tell Ourselves

*W*here did we get those t-shirts? Nobody can really remember where, or when, or even why. The big-hair wigs and sequined sunglasses we bought later at a costume shop, but the t-shirts came first. One of us—oh yes, it was Barbara—saw them, thought they were funny, and promptly bought six of them, one for each of us. As a joke. They were not meant to be our signature look. And they certainly weren't meant to be worn on stage in front of three hundred of our professional colleagues.

"Girls, I won't do this," said Lee, the oldest, and also the tallest. You'd think that as a former model standing nearly six feet tall, Lee would be used to being looked at. "But not like this," she said.

The thing was, those t-shirts were sexy. Very sexy. On the front was a woman's slinky, curvy body wearing a teeny tiny bikini. The shirt was made to look as if the painted body and bikini belonged to the wearer of the shirt. The front was bad enough, but the back was even worse. It had a woman's back with only a skinny thong

1

going up between her big round sassy cheeks. When you wore them, they looked real, particularly if you held them a little tight. When seen from a distance it looked like we were these exceptionally busty—and cheeky—Barbie look-alikes.

They were designed as humorous bathing suit cover ups, and became popular later, although at the time not many people had seen them. Especially not in Minneapolis, where the conference was being held.

We were, and are, professional business women working in the training, consulting and coaching industry. That's how we met. All of us were distributors of a particular set of assessment tools that we used in our work, and sold to others in the industry. The tools were Carlson Learning Company products, and it was at their annual business conference that we pondered whether to expose ourselves in our t-shirts, looking like "bad girls."

In reality, we were the furthest thing from bad girls you could find. That's probably why those t-shirts made us giggle so hard. How do you make a good girl giggle? Let her pretend to be bad. Works every time.

But display our silly bad girl side in public? Not so fast!

The idea began when Nicki, the youngest, read in the Carlson pre-conference brochure that the annual event that year would be a talent show. There was an application form to send in if you wanted to participate.

"I think we should do a song and dance lip-synch kind of thing," Nicki wrote in an email to the rest of us. "It'll be fun."

Gina's immediate email answer was, "Yes! Let's do it!" Gina can be counted on for go-for-it emotion. She's from a big Italian family and can't help herself. Nicki's of Italian descent too, and when the two of them get excited, it can be quite a show.

Lauri wrote a more measured email saying, "I'm game for whatever we want to do." But when Lauri is on board, we all know things will get done. She will make sure of it.

Susan didn't write back right away, because she likes to sit with ideas for a while before she agrees or disagrees. It's important for her to understand her motivations and whether the idea will serve a higher purpose. Susan is our spiritual rock. So when her email arrived saying, "Okay, let's get silly and have some fun," participating in the talent show looked like it was going to happen.

But then Nicki called Barbara, and Barbara said, "We can't do it if we all don't do it, and I know Lee won't do it." Barbara and Lee knew each other well, even though they had met only a couple of years before, just like the rest of us. They shared many similarities. For one thing, they were the oldest of us girls, both in their early fifties at that time. Both tall blondes, they looked so alike that many people got them mixed up. Most important, they were both strong leaders everyone looked up to.

In spite of Barbara's prediction, Nicki was sure she could persuade Lee, so she called her. Nicki had nicknamed Lee "Jackie O" because she reminded her of Jackie Onassis. "Lee's our matriarch," claimed Nicki. At first Lee didn't like it. "I'm not a matriarch!" she said indignantly. But Lee is 25 years older than Nicki and she saw Jackie O as the personification of glamour, so she finally accepted the nickname. Now she loves it, and even signs her emails (to us) "Jackie O."

"Jackie O!" said Nicki when she got Lee on the phone. "You've got to do this talent show with us. It'll be so much fun. We need you."

"Absolutely not," said Lee cheerfully.

"But Jackie O, why not?"

"Darling, I'm older than you," said Lee. "I've been there and done that. I've made a fool of myself too many times to do it again. And if I did do it again, it's not going to be at a professional event that we attend every year."

Nothing Nicki said would change her mind. So Nicki called Barbara back and said, "You're right, she's not going to do it. I guess we'll have to give it up."

But by this time Barbara had decided that *she* wanted to do it. At the time, Barbara and Lee both lived in Florida, so Barbara said, "No, sign us up. We're flying in together, and on the plane she won't have any escape. I'll get her 'liquored up' and she'll agree. Don't worry about it."

Nobody knows how Barbara did it, but when she and Lee got to Minneapolis, Lee was almost on board. Reluctantly, but she was at least halfway there.

And this is all before we decided to wear the t-shirts!

Those t-shirts were Barbara's fault. She brought them with her to Minneapolis. She said, "I just thought they might come in handy for the talent show." Well, she was right.

Another memory fog overcomes us when we try to remember who suggested we lip-synch the song *Bad Girls*, which was a Donna Sommer hit back in the seventies. Did we pick the song to match the t-shirts, or remember the t-shirts when we came up with the song? We can't remember.

It was probably Gina who suggested the song, though. She was a disco fiend back in the seventies when she was a teenager. We decided that she should be the lead singer in our routine, and the rest of us would be the doo-wop backup singers.

We wanted something bouncy and sexy, so we could gyrate our hips like the Supremes. We even thought about doing the Supremes, but we didn't have any tight spangled dresses. But hey, we did have t-shirts!

The song *Bad Girls* and our t-shirts seemed to fit together. When you listen to the lyrics, you realize that it's a pretty raunchy song. It's about prostitution, which of course is not a light subject at all. But the tempo is upbeat and strong, so maybe, we told ourselves, it was okay to sing it in a light-hearted vein. Donna Sommer did.

So there we were, six professional business women contemplating lip-synching a song about prostitutes and wearing t-shirts painted with nearly-naked boobs and butts in front of hundreds of people *who knew us* and had previously believed us to be serious people committed to helping others be successful. Lee was having a cow.

"We'll never live this down," she kept saying. "We'll be known as the fools of our profession forever."

But what if no one knew it was us? That was when we thought of wearing outrageous wigs and sequined sunglasses as disguise. (We added whistles too – listen to the song and you'll know why.) It made all of us feel safer, and Lee stopped waffling. She wasn't just on board, she was steering the boat.

"I'm so much taller than everyone else, my t-shirt doesn't go down as far," she mused. "Everyone else's stops at their knees – mine barely covers my butt." She looked at herself in the mirror.

"So that's it," she declared. "I'm not wearing jeans or slacks. I'm wearing black tights. If I'm going to wear this costume, I'm going to look as good as I possibly can." Lee has the great long legs of a fashion model. We all envied her those legs.

She tried the outfit on with the tights. "Nah," she said, "I think I'll take the tights off and just go bare." *Oh my god*, we all thought. *Lee's on the loose now.*

So now we had a song, a boom-box and cassette tape, and our costumes. We just needed a dance routine. Up in Barbara and Lee's hotel room, where we practiced, we tried to develop our routine ourselves. It was pretty bad at first. Mostly we kept falling over each other laughing.

Even though we were going to be singing and dancing incognito, we still wanted to be *good* as "Bad Girls." So we went on a recruiting mission to get some help, and came back with two colleagues we swore to secrecy. Josh was a friend of Barbara's from Florida. He had his own business like us but when he said he had done some theatre in the past, we scooped him up and let him know what we were doing. He became our choreographer, and he was great at planning out our dance steps and directing us to act out the song's story. "Turn around, girls. You gotta show more ass!" he kept saying, as well as "Sex it up! Sex it up!" This struck us as pretty funny because Josh was gay and we're pretty sure he didn't find us sexy at all.

The other colleague we roped in played the "john" in our production. His name was Jack and at the time he was Susan's business partner. He was a big player in our industry and we were all surprised when he said he'd help us out; it didn't look like his kind of thing. Jack was a guy who looked conservative and was. Yet he really got into his part, and while we were rehearsing he echoed Josh's repeated directions to "show more ass." "I'm interested in your bottom line," he said. He wasn't kidding. Later on we found out whose bottom he had his eye on, but at the time we didn't know that love was his motivating factor.

We almost lost our nerve when it was time for the actual show. We had stashed our costumes backstage, and when it was almost our turn we casually strolled out of the audience—not together, but one at a time—and went behind the curtains to get dressed. When we were dressed we looked at each other in all our cheap and wacky glory and wondered if maybe we should just sneak back out again. But then we heard the MC say, "Here come the Bad Girls," and we were onstage. Just like that.

To be honest, none of us remember the details of our performance. It went by in a blur. But we could tell the audience loved it. They laughed and clapped in all the right places, and by the end, we felt great.

After our performance, we went backstage and took off our costumes, scrubbed off our makeup, and snuck out the back door. Then we casually re-entered the hall at different times so nobody could put two and two together and realize that we were the Bad Girls.

And it worked! Nobody figured out that the Bad Girls were us. We overheard a lot of people asking, "Who were the Bad Girls?" as if we were the Lone Ranger or something. To our knowledge, no one knows they were us, even today.

It was probably a good thing we didn't win the talent show competition. We would have had to come clean. But we didn't even get an honorable mention. Oh well. Maybe it's because our talent was too amazing to believe. That's what we told ourselves, anyway.

But it really didn't matter. We felt like winners. Later on that evening, as we celebrated in the bar, we gave ourselves "low-fives," which are high-fives under the table.

————————▽————————

Who we are depends on which story we decide to tell ourselves. That's what this book is about—the stories we told ourselves in the past, and the stories we tell ourselves now.

Before the talent show, we called our little clique of six friends simply "the girls," but after the show we had a name for what we were to each other. We were the "bad girls."

The ironic thing is that we are not bad girls, not in the way society defines that term. All of us are do-gooders with a passion to help others and make the world a better place, as corny as that sounds. But we have embraced the term "bad girls" as our own because we are redefining "bad girls" as women who have the courage to break out of society's molds and define themselves in new ways. When we join together in solidarity, it doesn't matter what we call ourselves.

Who we are depends on which story we decide to tell ourselves. That's what this book is about—the stories we told ourselves in the past, and the stories we tell ourselves now.

Plus all the fun we have together.

Meet the Girls:
Gina, Lauri, Lee, Barbara, Susan, Nicki

TWO

Taking Big Chances

Our t-shirted debut as "the bad girls" was in 2001. But that was not the beginning of *us*. That was just our coming out party—a good time, but not nearly the whole story.

Our beginning as a powerful group of women who aimed to do good in the world, and do good for ourselves at the same time, was several years earlier.

How we all met is not an unusual story. We'd arrived via different paths, but we'd all ended up in the same industry. We are professional colleagues, which is a pretty normal way for people to meet. But what we became, now that was unusual.

Some would say that random chance brought us together, but we know better. We don't believe in random chance. We *do* believe in angels. And our angels were working overtime.

Why we clicked so fast was more than just being in the same industry, although it helped that our industry was motivational training. Our jobs are to help people become the best they can be, and synthesize what they do with who they are. We each thought we were pretty "together" in this regard—after all, we were the teachers!

That old adage "teach in order to learn" is old because it is true. Our angels knew that we had some new and magical things we needed to learn before we could train others. One of these is this: we are the stories we tell ourselves.

If we want to live productive, peaceful, joy-filled lives right now, we can. If we want to attract beautiful, adventurous, and fun-filled experiences into our futures, we can. Anyone can. It all depends on our stories—which *we* make up as we go along.

We can even rewrite the past. No, we have not discovered how to travel back to Cleopatra's time (What fun that would be!). But we can re-live our own past and change our reactions to the circumstances of that past. We can retell our own stories so our conclusions about past happenings are those that support and nurture us. We can do this if we have the willingness and support to step out into the unknown.

Angels love adventure. And they love stories. That's why they brought us together, so we could tell our stories to each other, and then share them with you.

Since all stories must begin somewhere, we'll start with how we met. Take it away, Barbara.

Chances Are: *Barbara*

1989 was a hard year for me. I was working for a travel company and I didn't like it. I was in the midst of an ugly divorce, and disliked that even more. Plus, I was struggling financially while helping support my three teenage sons on my meager sales earnings. Bottom line: I was tired!

I wanted to find something I could do that would be fun, not so much work, and pay me a lot of money. Fat chance! I had been taking care of myself for a long time, and I knew that what I wanted did not exist. My mother was a divorcee and single parent during the mid 1950s when divorce was a stigma. The only way to "take care of yourself" was to marry a man who would do it for you. I tried that route twice, and it didn't work for me either.

I'd had a mostly good marriage, and a mostly bad one. The bad one had just ended, and it left me alone and struggling. I wasn't sure I wanted another relationship, but I *was* sure I wanted a new career.

I had worked as a secretary for NBC in Manhattan, I'd been an assistant store manager at Bonwit Teller in Chicago, I'd owned and run a gift and novelty shop, and I'd worked as a travel agent. None of these occupations gave me everything I wanted; for one thing, they weren't enough fun! And none of them paid me enough, either. They did teach me that I was good at sales, because I loved helping people get their lives unstuck. Buy a beautiful dress, change your attitude, become unstuck. Go on an exotic vacation, change your outlook, become unstuck. But these fixes were temporary, and what I really wanted to sell was a way to help people become permanently unstuck.

The irony was that *my* life was stuck. I've never been able to stand being stuck. I like to move. I'd rather take a big chance than remain without a choice, even if the only choices are poor ones. I was 46 years old, only four years away from fifty, which at the time sounded old (Now 46 sounds young!). If I was going to change careers, I felt I had to change *before it was too late*.

Divine intervention was at hand. One day I was visiting with my son and a friend of his, and talking about my desire to change careers. "I was thinking of something in the motivation field," I said. My son's friend reached into his pocket and pulled out a business card. "My dad's friend gave me this card," he said. "He met this woman on a plane and she told him about her job selling motivational training tools. He thought it might be a good opportunity for me, but I'm not interested. So maybe you should check it out." And he gave me the business card.

I'd rather take a big chance than remain without a choice, even if the only choices are poor ones.

To be honest, I didn't believe this would lead anywhere. I stuck the card in my purse, thanked him and forgot about it.

It was Lauri's card. A few days later I found it in my purse and was going to throw it away, but then I thought, oh why not? So I called her even though I had no idea what I was calling about.

It was a strange conversation. Lauri was in high-speed mode (I learned later this mode was normal for her) because she had a plane to catch and was running late. (This was also normal for her.) She asked if she could call me back the next week, after the conference that was coming up.

"Could you just tell me something about the company quickly, before you run?" I asked.

"Okay," she said. "I've never been happier, never had more fun, and never made more money. Meanwhile, here's a number you can call to find out about the Carlson Learning Company conference that's coming up in Minneapolis. If you're interested, I'll sponsor you to come." And just like that, she hung up.

I felt as if a whirlwind had just blown through me. *She's never been happier, never had more fun, and never made more money. I think I'll go to that conference.*

And I did. It was a huge commitment, especially in terms of the money it cost, which I didn't have. Lauri, a woman I had never met and had just one swift conversation with, agreed to be my sponsor and put me in her "downline." I agreed to start my own training company so I could become a distributor of motivational training tools. Just like that.

My family and friends all told me I was crazy. "You need a real job with a regular salary," they said. "The last thing you should do is go out on your own." But I knew in my heart that this was exactly what I needed to be doing.

I wasn't stuck anymore.

Divine Intervention: *Lauri*

I barely remember that first phone conversation with Barbara. As she said, I was in a hurry that day. But I do remember meeting her at the Minneapolis conference a week later. There were hundreds of people attending, and I had no idea what Barbara looked like. I didn't know how I was going to find her; I couldn't peer at every name tag pasted on hundreds of chests. But I was her sponsor, which was a responsibility I took seriously. She didn't know a soul there, and she knew nothing about the company, the products, or even what her job was going to be. It wasn't just Barbara who had taken a chance; so had I.

If that wasn't enough to prove that something was going on,

Barbara and I clicked immediately. I felt as though I'd known her forever. She wanted to know the road I'd traveled to get to this place, and over dinner that night I found myself telling her much more than I usually told my business associates.

When I was a child I assumed I would become a teacher. That's what my mother wanted me to be, because that's what she wanted to be, and wasn't. My parents sacrificed a lot for my education, so I became a teacher. I taught high school English for years, and I did enjoy teaching kids to love their language and write it well. But it wasn't really me, although I didn't understand that then. For a woman, your career choices in the sixties and seventies were secretary, nurse, or teacher.

I married young, to a guy I admired when I was in high school. He was an engineering student in college. I followed him to Ohio State, and we married when I was a sophomore. After college he got a good job, as did I, and we had two children within five years. I was following the script that a good woman was supposed to follow. The seventies were a time when being a working mom was becoming more accepted, and I felt we were the perfect couple: religious, educated, ambitious and career-oriented. We moved around a lot because of his career; my job as a teacher took second place to his, which is how it was back then. I didn't question it, the same way I didn't question becoming a teacher.

In 1981 we moved again, and I couldn't find a full-time teaching position. I had too much experience for schools to put me on as a permanent teacher. That's when I met a businesswoman who introduced me to the field of corporate training. She needed assistance in traveling and training for her business-writing company. I loved corporate training, and my sheltered world expanded. I learned sales techniques and traveled across the country to trade shows, standing in front of major corporations teaching employees how to write letters, memos, proposals and reports. Business education was a world I never knew existed. Here I was, "Lauri the school teacher" in an exciting, fast-paced business world. I embraced it and became part of it. I taught in the conference rooms of impressive corporate offices, traveled throughout the country, rented cars in strange cities, stayed in hotels by myself, and most of all, worked with grown-ups who seemed to believe that I fit in.

I did this job part-time for several years, traveling about three days a week. My two children were in junior high and high school, so it worked out fine for my family. Then through a friend of my husband, I met a woman who was a manager for General Motors. She asked me if I'd be interested in applying for a contract teaching position.

"I don't even know what a spark plug does," I said. I didn't think she was serious. But she said, "If you pass the interviews and assessment tests, we'll teach you everything you need to know."

General Motors flew me up to Flint, Michigan for an entire day of interviews finalized by requiring me to make a stand-up presentation. GM supplied the audience, complete with a bunch of jerks who deliberately tried to be distracting. That was their job.

I guess I handled them appropriately because GM told me I had the skills they were looking for, despite my lack of an automotive background. I began traveling all over the country on different contract positions. I met other professional trainers who recommended me for different contracts. I joined Carlson Learning Company as a distributor, selling training products, which I used in my work. I got paid a bonus when I signed up others to be distributors too—people like Barbara. Ultimately, I became one of the movers and shakers at annual conferences. These business conferences were stimulating and exciting. I met many professionals who encouraged, educated and supported me. I was experiencing a dream career.

I've never been happier, never had more fun, and never made more money.

A few years later, after working for several automotive companies as a contract trainer, Chrysler hired me as one of six trainers to secure training professionals for a customer service project. Chrysler needed seventy new trainers who'd travel nationwide to train senior management and over 200,000 retail automotive people on customer service and new management techniques. I was able to introduce many of the trainers, including Barbara, who I'd met at the Carlson conferences to the automotive training world. It felt good to give others a great financial opportunity as had been done for me years before. Sometimes we met the executives on private jets to pitch our ideas. Chrysler's "Customer One" was a forty-million dollar project, the largest automotive training project done to date in the industry; and it was a long, long way from grading high school English papers. Sometimes I would look around and think, *how can this be me? I don't deserve this.* But it was me, and I must have deserved it. Otherwise I wouldn't have it, right?

That's how I got into motivational training, and my professional life had never been better. My personal life was a little rockier, but it cemented my burgeoning friendship with Barbara when we discovered—the first night we met—that we were both going through difficult times in our personal lives. By the end of that 1989 conference, I had two new friends, Barbara and Lee, another first-timer attending the conference. Barbara and Lee could have been sisters. They're both tall slender blondes with unique smiles that are just a little crooked and more than a little contagious. And laughs that fill your heart.

Whether I deserved them or not, I knew they were in my life for good.

Somebody: *Lee*

Although I was a new distributor of Carlson products in 1989, I'd been doing sales and motivational training for over twenty years by then. But I was excited about the products and looking forward to the conference even though I knew no one. I love meeting new people.

I thought I must have looked pretty darn good that first day of the conference, because people kept coming up to me and chatting away, as if they knew who I was and liked me a lot. Then I noticed that many of them thought my name was Barbara.

I learned later that the same thing had been happening to Barbara, who people mistook for me. We both were thinking, "Who is this person, and where is she?"

At the conference orientation meeting for first-timers, I got there a little early so I could sit in the front row. The speaker got up and said, "Let's meet each other. Turn around and say hi to the person behind you." I turned around and there was Barbara, directly behind me. I knew her instantly.

"You're Barbara!" I said, exactly at the same time she burst out, "You're Lee!"

We laughed, and even our laughs were alike. We jabbered at each other all through the orientation. We tried to keep quiet, but I don't think we did a very good job. People kept looking at us, as if we were twins who had been separated at birth and had just been reunited. Actually, that's pretty much what it felt like. After the orientation, we wandered off to the bar together, then we had dinner, and I don't think we stopped talking until we finally had to go to bed around midnight.

The more we talked, the more similarities we discovered. It would have been spooky if it hadn't felt so natural. We each had all sons and no daughters. We each had two sisters and no brothers. We were around the same age (Okay, I'm a few years older). We had both been through a divorce. And of course we had the same jobs as training consultants, although Barbara was just starting out and I had been doing various kinds of training for years.

I love the spotlight, always have. That's where my energy comes from, and I always thought I would be on stage. When I was a little girl, I would go to the Saturday matinees at the movie theatre in our Detroit neighborhood. I went all by myself, and sat there all day. I earned the money for my ticket, popcorn and jujubes by carrying people's groceries home for them during the week, loading them in my little red wagon. It was hard work for a child, but I didn't mind, because it meant that on Saturday I could live inside my dream. It was the late 1940s and Marge and Gower

Champion sang and danced their way into my heart. I knew I was meant to be on stage, too.

Unfortunately, I couldn't sing or dance. It took me some time to realize this. Somehow I convinced my mother to let me take singing lessons. They didn't last long because the instructor told my mother (with me listening), "There's no hope for her. Please do me a favor and don't bring her back."

Well, what did he know? So I tried out for the church choir when I was around eleven or twelve. They put me in the front row at first, because I was "such a pretty girl." But then I gradually started moving back, finally ending up in the back row. Eventually the choir director told me gently that singing was not my thing.

And as for dancing—I was tall and skinny and had two left feet. Even I knew that dancing was beyond me. So much for my dreams of being Somebody.

I'm sure my parents were relieved when I gave up my dream of being a singer. My parents were modest, conservative folks, and the worst sin in their world was "showing off." They were always concerned that I was too full of myself, or stuck-up. "Remember, you're nobody special," they'd tell me. They had to tell me that a lot, because I didn't want to believe them. Besides, if you're a woman nearly six feet tall, you will stand out. There's no way to avoid it. So why not go with it?

My parents' relief was short-lived, because after I graduated from high school at 17, I decided to go to modeling school. I never had a desire to go to college; I'd been brought up to believe that college was for boys. Girls were supposed to work for a while, and then get married and have babies. Your whole goal as a woman was to take care of your husband and children. You were supposed to remain in the background of your own life.

So modeling was not what my parents wanted for me. Being a model means your job *is* showing off. It was a requirement of modeling school that you enter beauty pageants, so that's what I did—more showing off. My parents never attended a pageant. They were too embarrassed. Even when I won or placed, they never once mentioned it to anyone.

It was from modeling that I got my first hint of what my work in the world was to become. After graduating, I became a professional fashion model, and then the modeling school hired me to teach other girls how to be models. I discovered two things: I was good at training, and I loved it. When you're training, peoples' eyes are on you. You're at the front of the room. It's a kind of stage, isn't it?

But perhaps to mollify my parents for my outrageous (in their eyes) career choice, I got married at 21, to a man twelve years older than me, and every bit as conservative as my parents. We began having children right away, and by the time I was 26 we had four sons.

Well, there went my modeling career, and you might think my dreams of being on a stage were dead too, but when you're born to stand out, you just find a way. I found the direct selling industry.

Direct selling—or home parties—is perfect for a young mother who wants to keep her sales skills honed. I'd be with the kids all day, and after they went to bed, I'd be out doing my parties and making extra money. The first company I worked for was called Beeline Fashions; it was Tupperware with clothes. It combined modeling with sales, and boy was I good at it. Many evenings I'd be drinking coffee and eating dessert with a group of women until

1 a.m., while counting the money I made that night in my head. My sales were so good that within a year I was made a manager so I could train other consultants to sell.

And then Avon came calling. We had moved to Cleveland so I had to leave Beeline and was looking for another direct selling opportunity. Avon was a gold mine for me. I was hired to manage a district of about 150 Avon ladies. My goals were to help these ladies learn how to sell, and to recruit new Avon ladies and teach them how to sell. We became the top-selling district in Ohio. We won awards and contests, and I became semi-famous within Avon. They finally promoted me to a level where women had never been before. Up until then, all the executives were men.

I was made a division manager and had 21 districts and district managers reporting to me—over 4,000 Avon ladies. I loved the job, but the problem was I was still married to this sweet man who wanted his wife to stay home, make cookies and take care of the babies. He never really accepted the fact that I even had a career. He was embarrassed about it, and especially embarrassed by my success. I was managing 4,000 people, traveling to New York and Los Angeles, and making more money than he was. But he would tell people that Avon was my hobby, "because she just likes the products."

It wasn't his fault. You can't blame someone for being a member of his own generation. He was a great dad to our four wonderful sons, and we had a good relationship for many years. But he wanted a comfortable background cozy type of wife. Instead he got me.

The end of our marriage came when I was offered a chance to work for another direct-selling company. They wanted to send me to Australia and build an all-female sales organization. My goal was to recruit 1,000 women in 18 months to build the company from the bottom up. Because of my success with Avon, I was well-known in the industry and they wanted me badly. They offered to pay for just about everything, even travel expenses for the kids back and forth between Australia and the US. They also promised a huge bonus if I achieved my goals.

I took the job. It was the right thing to do, but it was the hardest decision I ever made. My sons were teenagers, and I worked it so their lives were disrupted as little as possible. In fact, they had a wonderful time in Australia during the summer they lived with me. And I achieved my goals, had a fantastic time in Australia, and got my bonus—plus a promotion to Vice President of Sales, Training and Development when I came back to the US.

I moved to their headquarters in New England. My job was building the sales organization, which consisted of 20,000 people at the time. It was an international company, so I traveled all over the world. It was my job to rally the troops, and I was always on stage somewhere. As you might guess, I loved this job, too.

I got married again, to a man who was proud of my business success, probably because he was a successful executive himself. I acquired two great step-children. The marriage was good for years, until we decided to move to Florida, where we had a vacation home. Eventually I went into business for myself, building a sales and motivation training program which became highly successful. But my husband did not do well outside of corporate America. He became depressed. At the time I became a Carlson Learning Products distributor and attended that first conference where I met Barbara and Lauri, my second marriage was on the rocks. Something both of them understood.

Coincidence? I hardly think so.

Yes, I love the spotlight. But sometimes it can feel lonely, all by yourself up there at the front of the room. It's lonely being one of the few women at the top. Being somebody is great, but I discovered that by sharing the spotlight with women like me, I could become somebody even better.

Being somebody is great, but I discovered that by sharing the spotlight with women like me, I could become somebody even better.

For a year after that first conference, Barbara and I kept in touch by phone (this was before email). She visited me in Florida, and I came to see her in Chicago. We talked about business, of course, but mostly we just made each other feel good. Barbara asked me for business advice, which made me feel like (what else) somebody. I cheered with her when she was able to tell her family, who had been against her starting her own business, that she made over $100,000 her first year. We listened to each other's stories about the agonies of divorce. We giggled, we sobbed, and we were there for each other.

We eagerly awaited the next business conference in 1990. We would have been even more eager if we'd known there was another person set to join our little group. Someone who would bring a spiritual dimension that would enhance us still further.

Divine Intervention, butting in again.

Flower Power: *Susan*

In 1990, I was doing what I'd been doing for the past ten years of my professional life: leadership training. We call it leadership or motivational training, but what does that really mean? At its core, it's teaching people to be more loving toward each other. It's all about trying to make the world a better place by enhancing people's self-esteem.

I've been seeking ways to save the world ever since I can remember. I don't know where this desire came from. My parents were not any kind of activists; both were conservative hard working people who held traditional values common to most people in Oklahoma, where I grew up. My childhood dream was to be Annie Oakley, because I loved horses and she was the only cowgirl I knew. My mother's goal for me was to go to college to get married. I was aware that there seemed to be something missing, but as a sheltered small-town Oklahoma girl, I had no idea what it could be.

That all changed when my father, a litigation attorney, moved us to New York in 1969. We lived there while I was fourteen and fifteen. This was during the heyday of the hippie era, and New York was in the heart of it. Peace and love and flowers sprouting from gun barrels. A longing to make the world a kinder, gentler place.

I became a "closet hippie." Because of my conservative upbringing, I didn't embrace the more outrageous aspects of that era, the free sex and the drugs, but in my heart I believed in all the social causes that made the sixties what they were: equal rights for everyone, an end to stupid wars, and no more greed, racism, or poverty. All you need is love. With a group of girlfriends, I wrote poetry, lit candles, and made paper flowers to hand out on the street, all while listening to Bob Dylan, Joan Baez, and Joni Mitchell. The only thing missing was the marijuana.

I came alive in New York. It brought me an awareness of who I really was and have always been at my core. I've never lost it.

But we went back to Oklahoma, and I floundered for a while. I knew I wanted to make a difference, but I had no idea how. I didn't want to be a radical and fight all the time. I knew how to fight, though; my father taught me. His job was to argue in court, and he was very good at it, so good that he liked to keep arguing at home. He had little tolerance for opposing viewpoints, but one good thing that came from this is that he taught me how to stand up and fight for what I thought was right. I didn't always win, especially with him, but it was arguing with him that gave me the persistence to stand in my own truth.

In search of whatever that truth was, I went off to a business college. I had to live in a dormitory, which meant I had no freedom. I hated it. And since I had no clear goals, I did poorly in school. So I quit, and went to work as a secretary in a law firm. There I was bored and the thought that kept running through my head was, "There's got to be more to life than this."

I went back to school, and like many, the second time I went to college I did better. In fact, I was a straight A student. I was more motivated, because I had found what I wanted to do: get a degree in Social Work so I could at last help make the world a better place.

I got my chance to help the world when my mother was diagnosed with breast cancer. This was in the seventies, and there was little support for women fighting cancer. After seeing what my mom went through, I organized a cancer support group. It was one of the first of its kind. My mother attended mainly because she saw it was so important to me. The group became a success; it was officially recognized and sponsored by the hospital. It also got me an A when I wrote it up as my term project. But on the night of the first kick-off of this program, my mother died.

I was 21 and far from saving the world. I had failed to save my own mother. It was at this time of grief that I won a scholarship to go to England and study at Oxford during the last semester before I received my undergraduate degree. I did a practicum in London at the Centre for Urban Studies. I loved the adventure and sense of expansion I felt. It was a much bigger world than I had known before in my small Oklahoma town.

After graduation, I didn't want to come home. It didn't feel like I had a home. My dad had remarried, and he and I were not close anyway. My mom was the one I was close to, and she was dead.

The problem was money. I had none. Eventually I landed in Amsterdam, supporting myself by working in a health food restaurant in exchange for room and board, and teaching yoga to pay for everything else. I got up at five in the morning to teach early morning yoga classes, worked all day in the health food restaurant, and went to bed at nine. Here I was living in the Sin City of Europe, where prostitution was legal and drugs were everywhere, and I wouldn't even let a hamburger touch my lips.

I went home to Oklahoma when I got tired of being poor in Europe. I had a degree in social work by this time, and I easily found a job at the Lung Association teaching non-smoking classes and lobbying for the Clean Air Act. Then a friend of mine from the University of Oklahoma got a grant to create DUI schools for teenagers, the number one cause of death for that age group. He decided to start a business, and offered me a partnership which I accepted. It was my job to create the training program.

I loved training. I went back to school to get my Masters in human relations and organizational development, and in a few years I decided to go out on my own. I still wanted to train, but I wanted a different focus. Social work tends to be depressing. You have to give up part of yourself. I looked around at my peers, and they weren't happy. Psychologists and psychiatrists have a high rate of suicide. Doctors have a high rate of drug dependency. I wanted to make the world better, but I also wanted to be happy doing it.

My goal was to work with healthy people who wanted to make their lives better. I was able to buy into a distributorship with a motivation institute. They trained me to sell their products to individuals and businesses. I trained my clients in a program that included visualizations and affirmations, everything in a positive vein. I loved it. People were happy. I was happy.

I ended up being in the top one percent of their distributors nationwide. I spoke at their conferences. I was on the front of their magazine. I guess you could say I was successful.

Then I moved to Chicago because of a man I'd met at a spiritual conference. I continued doing the training thing, and again I was successful – although the relationship I moved for was a different story. It was in Chicago that I met Lauri. She recruited me into being a Carlson distributor. There were several of us who were selected to work closely with Carlson Learning Company, and she and I were given the Chicago area to share. Lauri was a kick to work with. She was very driven, and also very funny. I loved the way she could talk a mile a minute, yet always make sense.

When the 1991 conference was coming up, Lauri told me about these two women she'd met the previous year—how funny they were, how smart, how warm, how this, how that. By the time I got to the conference, I was curious to meet Barbara and Lee.

They were everything Lauri claimed they were. In fact, they were more. I hadn't expected to find a spiritual community waiting for me in the midst of a professional conference. But here they were, three women just like me: spiritual beings in a commercial world.

Although they didn't think of themselves that way. "I'm not very spiritual," Lee told me, which made me laugh. This woman glowed with light. "I'm just a normal person, nothing special about me," said Lauri, as she did fifteen things at once, all perfectly. "I don't think I'm very deep; I just like to have fun," said Barbara, as she accepted each of us exactly as we were, and loved us completely.

You don't have to know you are doing spiritual work in order to do it. You just have to be who you truly are. Together we were creating a space for each of us to become spiritually whole. But we weren't complete yet. There were two more yet to come, and the holes would all be filled.

I can hardly wait to share what happened next.

Home in the World: *Gina*

Although my title—Corporate Director of Training—sounded pretty impressive, I hadn't been doing training long when I was introduced to Carlson products in 1992. Actually, I made my business title up and convinced corporate management to let me have it.

I worked for a management corporation which ran various resorts and hotels. I worked my way up by doing virtually every job there was in the hospitality industry. I only completed two years of college, and did not get a degree, because I saw myself as a worker bee—someone who always had a good job and never had to worry about money. The hospitality industry, especially hotels and resorts, is a good place for worker bees. They'll let you work as much as you want and then ask you to work more. I was always looking for different avenues to work more and work harder. I was a concierge manager. I worked in the restaurant. I worked in banquets. I worked in catering. Eventually I became the Director of Guest Services, right before I talked myself into the training job.

My training career began when two other managers and I were required to take a hospitality and guest relations training course, so we could train all the other managers and many employees on the same thing. We all got certified, but the other two managers, both men, never seemed to have time to train anyone else. It was left up to me.

That was okay, though, because I discovered I loved training. I could relate to the people I trained because I had done what they did, whether it was washing dishes, changing beds or scrubbing toilets, as well as the front end jobs like concierge. It didn't matter to me what someone's actual job was. What I loved about training was it was really about showing people practical ways to be nice to one another. In short, I taught friendliness. How could you not like that?

Eventually I went to the president of the company and told him he needed to create a job for me, and call it Corporate Director of Training. It took me six months to convince him, including doing a stint as the manager of the hotel restaurant, but he finally agreed.

The thing was, the title might have been impressive, but the money was about the same as I had been making for years. And although I loved the work, there was a lot more of it. Sometimes it seemed like all I did was work.

I was based at an upscale resort outside of Chicago. One afternoon in 1992 I had made an appointment with a representative selling a training program I was considering for the hotel's management team. The representative was Barbara.

We met in the lobby of the resort, and I know it sounds corny, but as soon as I met her I felt I'd known her forever. She has a way of looking at you—really looking into you—that makes you feel as if she knows all about you. But it isn't intimidating, because at the same time you feel as if she really *likes* who you are. She projects total acceptance, and I wish I could figure out how she does it.

I had allotted thirty minutes for the appointment, but we were in that lobby much longer than that, drinking tea and talking nonstop about a lot more than her training programs. Our conversation went personal within five minutes. At the time I was single and on a dating extravaganza. Barbara was fifteen years older than me, but she too was single and dating a lot, and there are few things richer, or funnier, to talk about than dating.

When we did talk business, I asked more questions about her job than her products, and in the end I didn't even purchase her training program. Instead she recruited me into selling them myself.

Actually, I recruited myself. I wanted what Barbara had—a chance to make good money and do what I loved, without killing myself with work in the process. And Barbara seemed to think I could do it.

Barbara came along at just the right time, when I'd been itching for a change. But I think it was more than the right time. It was meeting the right person who could give me the courage to take a big chance.

I've always been a play-it-safe kind of person. I grew up in a large, warm, noisy Italian family, surrounded by the protection that only a close family can give you. I was the oldest of four children, with an extended family of grandparents, aunts, uncles and cousins always around too. My parents were hard-working, blue-collar, old-fashioned and conservative. They lived their values and insisted we live them too. The reward was lots and lots of love. Warm arms around you whenever you needed them. Constant company so you were never lonely. Someone always at your back.

But of course it wasn't perfect. My parents tended to be overprotective. For instance, when we were children, none of us had bicycles. All our friends had them; I used to watch them zooming down the streets. They looked so free. But as a child my father had seen his cousin hit and killed by a truck while he was riding a bicycle. Therefore Dad *knew* bikes were dangerous, and he passed that fear on to us kids. It wasn't just bicycles; Dad knew there were many things that could hurt his beloved children. He was cautious and protective. God rest his soul.

While I was growing up, my family would probably have been classified as poor. All of my siblings, three girls and one boy, slept in the same bedroom until we were teenagers. Things got a little better then, and my parents were able to buy a nice little house—which was always crammed with family, of course.

I didn't feel poor, exactly. We had food and clothes and all the essentials. It was just that whenever I wanted to do something extra—like join the Girl Scouts, or dance class—I couldn't do it because there wasn't enough money. "If you're smart and you work hard, you can do anything you want," my mother told me. That's why I worked so hard. I remember thinking, "When I grow up, I'm going to make sure I have a good job so I will have money."

My mother worked outside the home, which was unusual for her generation, and a source of embarrassment for my father. He hated that she worked at night, even though during the day she watched the children, made the dinner and cared for the house. He especially hated the kind of work she did. She was—and still is today—a nightclub singer. She sings a lot of Barbra Streisand and Judy Garland songs that are sensual, sultry, earthy and full of love and longing—and sometimes just a little raunchy humor. Oh, we all loved to hear my mother sing, even though I was an adult before I heard her really belt it out at a nightclub.

There were two great things my mother's unusual job taught me. First of all, I learned how to be responsible when I was a child. Since I was the oldest I took care of my younger sisters and brother, and I learned how to manage a home when my mother wasn't there. Secondly, and even more important, she showed me that you could spread joy in the world by doing what you love. You could sing your heart out to total strangers, and then come home again. It took me so long to learn this lesson because I had to learn it by doing it myself.

In fact, I didn't really learn it until I got to know Barbara, Lauri, Lee, Susan, and Nicki.

I love what my parents gave me, that feeling of warmth and protection and home, where you are safe and loved. I wanted, and still want, to keep that for myself and pass it down to my own child. I just didn't want the fear that came along with it. But until I met Barbara and the rest of the girls, I thought it was a package deal. I didn't know you could be safe and still take a chance. I didn't know you could make the whole world your home.

That's what I saw in Barbara. It wasn't just the training products she was selling, or the company that made those products. It was that she was warm and safe and full of adventure and excitement, too. And if she could have both these things, so could I. Like my mother, I could take my joy out into the world.

I didn't know you could be safe and still take a chance.

So instead of selling me the training program for my hotel, Barbara sold me on changing careers. I became a Carlson distributor, selling their products to clients I found myself, and training them to use them. For the first time in my life—I was in my early thirties then—I traveled by myself. Believe it or not, I had never been on an airplane, in a car, or on a bus alone. And here I was traveling not just to different cities, but to different states! All by myself.

At the next annual Carlson Learning Company conference, I met Lauri, Susan and Lee, and another newbie that Barbara had recruited, Nicki. Every one of them was professional and accomplished and full of light and love. As soon as I met them, they were family.

Even though only Nicki was Italian.

Yes We Can: *Nicki*

In 1994, I was at loose ends, not sure what I wanted to do, actually doubtful of what I could do. I had just lost my sales job due to downsizing, and personally, I wasn't sure what I was looking for in a relationship. For the first time in my life, I felt it was a challenging time.

Then my sister was getting married. She was happy, and since I loved my sister, I was happy for her. I just wished I could be happy for me.

Weddings are a social time, especially for my family. We are a big Irish-Italian-American clan and very Chicago. My mother is the Irish one, but she acted more Italian than the Italians—probably in self-defense.

There were lots of parties. At one such party, I found myself talking to the mother of the groom, my sister's future mother-in-law. I didn't know her well, other than she was a successful career woman and beautiful to boot, with a warm manner and a crooked smile that made you want to smile back. She was Barbara.

Making small talk, I asked her what she did for a living. She told me. It sounded great—she was making money and making people happy at the same time. "And I'm having so much fun!" she laughed.

"I want to do what you do!" I blurted out.

"Why not?" she said. "I'd love to show you how."

Why not? What a good question. I had lots of answers.

I never did that well in school, for one thing. Growing up, my sister was the smart one. I was the social one. We're best friends, but we're nothing alike. When my mom would tell us to clean up our room, I'd suggest we just shove everything under the bed or in the closet so we could get out and play with our friends. My sister would draw a diagram of our bedroom and make a plan on how best to arrange it and keep it clean. By the time she was done, I was hopping all over the room with impatience. Had I known she'd grow up to be an interior designer, I probably would have been more in-tune with her plans.

I nicknamed my sister "Larry King" because she asked so many questions. She likes to know how things work and why they work the way they do. I just accept whatever people tell me; I have little intellectual curiosity. Recently my mom called me and said, "We're going to make the Easter raviolis on Saturday. Call your sister and be here at 10 a.m.."

I said, "Okay," and called my sister.

"Why are we doing it on Saturday?" she said.

"I don't know, it's what Mom said."

"Why 10 a.m.?"

"I don't know, it's what Mom said."

"Are we making anything besides raviolis?"

"I don't know. Mom didn't say."

When I was a kid thinking about what I wanted to be when I grew up, I saw myself owning my own restaurant. I love to cook, and I love to entertain. I love a lot of people around, all having a good time. I saw myself as the owner of a big family-style Italian restaurant, coming out from the kitchen to greet my guests, wearing a tomato-gravy spattered apron and smiling.

But I also had a secret desire to be a teacher, even though school was hard for me. I kept this dream secret because I knew it could never come true. To be a teacher, you had to be smart and graduate from college. People said I was smart, but I never believed them. I did manage to get my Associate's degree, but every day was a struggle. I decided not to go on because it was clear that school was just not my thing.

As for the restaurant dream, I had learned by then that the restaurant business is mostly very hard work, leaving little time for socializing. So I joined the working world by taking a job with the police department. I started as a community service officer, which was a civilian position (meaning I didn't have to go to the Police Academy—another school), and from there I became a telecommunications officer, or a dispatcher.

I loved being a dispatcher. It played to my strengths, because it was all about working with and helping people. I answered emergency and non-emergency calls, and the job really kept me on my toes. I could have ten people calling about the same traffic accident they witnessed and get ten different descriptions of ten different intersections. I spoke with agitated people and calmed them down. I patiently sorted out their stories. I instructed them on what to do and what not to do so they'd be safe.

When I started with the police department, there was only one female officer. Many people expected me to be the next one. But I realized early on that I did not want to be a police officer, for the simple reason that I'm afraid of my own shadow.

People never believe me when I tell them I'm a chicken-hearted girl. I'm only 5'1" and to compensate I sometimes put on a tough show. But honestly, I cannot imagine going into a building at midnight to check out a burglar alarm going off. Just the thought that there might be a real burglar inside would make me freeze up. I'd be an awful cop.

It wasn't just physical courage I lacked, but confidence on so many levels. I'm typically about twenty pounds overweight, maybe to make myself look bigger, but it actually hurts my confidence instead. It just makes me think I'm unattractive. People told me it wasn't true, but I didn't believe them about that either.

Eventually I left the police department and decided to enter the sales field, and ended up working for a variety of organizations in several different industries. I was good at sales because I loved building relationships and working with people. My mom often said I could sell my way out of a paper bag, so it seemed a good fit for my personality. People seemed to like me too, although I always thought I was too loud and emotional. Nobody has any trouble believing I'm Italian. My mom is the calm one in our family. She's a breast cancer survivor. When I was around 21, Mom told us, "Okay, so I've been diagnosed with breast cancer, and this is what we're going to do. We're going to get through this, and everyone will be okay." She was right. She never wavered, she never broke down. She just did what she had to do, and she survived. I was the one who cried.

So I believed I had all these faults. I didn't do well in school. I'm loud and emotional. I'm overweight. I'm a chicken. And here was Barbara, telling me that of course I would be great at selling training products and teaching people how to use them! She told me she was impressed with my guts. Guts? *Get outta here!*

But there's something about Barbara that makes you believe her. And besides, I needed a job, and here was a successful, professional, together woman telling me she knew I could do it.

So I put on my competent face, and went for it even though I was scared inside. I became a distributor of training products and tools, and began learning the ropes of the learning and development industry. I even started my own training business. Little did I know it would be the growth I was looking for. I could make a six figure income and have fun!

Divine Intervention brought us together— so we could tell ourselves new and better stories, and grow together.

The following year I attended the annual conference, and met Lauri, Lee, Susan, and Gina. I looked up to all these successful professional women, all of them older than me, better educated than me, more experienced than me.

Why did I believe them when they told me of course I would be successful, when I hadn't believed others earlier in my life? It wasn't because I thought they were better than me. It was because they convinced me they *weren't* better than me.

In their essence, their stories were just like mine. That's why Divine Intervention brought us together—so we could tell ourselves new and better stories, and grow together.

Here's to Divine Storytelling.

Supporting Each Other in Business and Friendship

THREE

We Can Handle The Truth

*I*t started as another one of Lauri's "adventures." Our group of six in 1994 was becoming familiar with these. Lauri seemed to have a knack for finding transformational opportunities. She is one of Divine Intervention's best agents.

We were attending another conference, improving our business skills and at the same time deepening our relationships with one another. Although we didn't know it then, we were about to take them way deeper than we'd ever dreamed.

"Girls, there's a demonstration of a new self help technique called *The Enrichment Process*™," Lauri informed us. "It sounds interesting—they say this technique can help people change their lives for the better. We should go."

We were always game to improve ourselves, so we went to the demonstration. At first it sounded a little on the "woo-woo" side. Lee summed it up when she whispered, "This is spooky!"

Spooky or not, we stayed. *The Enrichment Process*™ is difficult to define in words because, as the name implies, it is an experiential process. Describing it is sort of like telling a joke that falls flat because to understand the joke "you had to be there." Nevertheless, we're going to try, because this technique became one of the most

43

important tools that enabled us to develop our unique bond.

The presenters didn't waste time explaining the psychological principles or theory behind the technique. They just did it. It's not that there isn't an explanation of why *The Enrichment Process*™ works; of course there is. It's just that you probably won't believe the reasoning until you experience the results. And because you don't believe it, there's a good chance you'll sabotage it. Basically, you had to try it to get it.

We watched the facilitator and a volunteer participant walk through a session. At first it looked like many other self-help practices; the participant identified and briefly discussed an aspect of her life she wanted to change. It wasn't an earth-shaking problem; just that she wanted to get along better with one of her co-workers. That's where the technique got a little "spooky."

None of us had heard of muscle testing before. The facilitator explained that our bodies don't forget, and they don't lie, either. Muscle testing can reveal hidden information about issues dealing with emotional and physical strengths, weaknesses, and desires. For instance, if you say, "I want to ask for a raise," your muscle system will weaken slightly if you actually believe that you don't deserve a raise, or you believe that asking for what you want is wrong. The signal from your muscle does not mean that your statement is true or false. It does not mean that it is good or bad for you to ask for a raise. It simply means that you have a belief that is contrary to your statement. This signal is critical because it creates the opportunity to align your beliefs with your desires.

Muscle testing looks easy, which is probably one reason why it seems like magic. The participant simply extends her arm out in front of her, keeping her elbow straight and arm rigid so it will resist downward pressure. The facilitator then grasps the participant's extended hand at the wrist, pointing his or her first and second fingers up the arm. The facilitator pushes down on the arm after the participant makes a statement. You have to be a trained facilitator to know how much pressure to apply.

If the statement is "true" at a deep level of belief, the participant's arm will remain rigid and in place. If the statement is "false," the participant's arm will weaken and the facilitator will be able to push the arm down. This is true no matter what the participant "thinks" the answer should be, or even if the participant does not "know" the answer.

During the demonstration, the facilitator and participant worked their way through some positive statements, muscle testing to see what was really true in the participant's mind. During the session they went back in time, dredging up memories from when the participant was a young child—because so many of our beliefs about ourselves stem from long ago. Watching this technique unfold, it made a huge impression on us that the participant looked so surprised as she remembered an incident from many years ago. That painful period had not existed in her consciousness since she was ten years old, but the beliefs engendered during that time were still there.

After they found the source of her non-productive beliefs, they worked on exchanging this belief for a more productive one. This involved more "woo-woo," although by this time we had given up most of our skepticism. The facilitator asked the participant to stand up, in order to keep her spine as straight as possible. She was asked to close her eyes and tap lightly with her fingertips on her sternum, which is the bone in the middle of your chest. The facilitator told us that there have been many theories why this steady tapping helps the mind and body leave old thoughts and vibrations behind, but all that's really known is that transformation is faster and easier when you do.

While continuing to tap, she was asked to visualize herself operating out of her new belief now and in the future, to think about specific actions she'd take, and where she'd be when she took them. She was asked to notice her body language, the smells, sounds, and physical sensations of the experience. This process continued for a few minutes, until she said she felt positive and satisfied with her new way of believing and thinking.

Those are the bare bones of *The Enrichment Process*™. It sounds simple, but that participant *changed*. We could see it in her face. We had no doubt that her life would now be different. It's difficult to convey how much that short demonstration fired us up; we were hooked from that point on. Barbara immediately signed up for facilitator training, and it wasn't long after she started working with her clients—and us—that the rest of us followed her. It wasn't just for our clients; it was for us. We felt an overwhelming rush of understanding that we needed to help ourselves more than we were already doing.

We brought the original facilitators in from Phoenix to Chicago so they could do an intensive weekend workshop for the six of us, plus others from the demonstration who had been introduced to it. After this workshop, we began holding what we called "processing parties" at Barbara's office, implementing what came to be called *The Enrichment Process*™ ourselves. Barbara became so proficient that she eventually purchased the rights to this human technology from the originators.

In short, we became process junkies. We processed all the time, from anywhere we could. Susan was especially persistent; we'd get together and do some sessions, and before we went home she'd be asking when we could get together to do more. It's not an exaggeration to say that we were in love with this new tool. And through the insights it gave us, we began to love each other, too.

―――――▽―――――

Each of us was working on ourselves individually, but working as a group was what created the tremendous closeness. We came to know each other so well, right down to our DNA.

All of us were going through intense situations in our own lives during this time. The technique allowed us to access our inner wisdom, and use the nurturing support the group gave us to implement that wisdom. To say *The Enrichment Process*™ brought us closer together is a vast understatement. When you work with this technique, you become very vulnerable. You are open to change and growth. Each of us was working on ourselves individually, but working as a group was what created the tremendous closeness. We came to know each other so well, right down to our DNA.

One of the many wonderful things about *The Enrichment Process*™ is that it results in psychological, emotional and spiritual benefits, yet it works on the physical plane. It actually shows you what to do and how to do it. This gave us an easy-to-follow, practical method of making our lives magical. One of its most interesting aspects is that at a certain point the process just takes off. It accesses the archives of your subconscious and your "knowing" guides you to the results you want to achieve.

To tell you the truth, even with all our training we still don't know why it works. We just know that it does.

And just to show you, we'll share some of our most magical moments.

Good Enough: *Lauri*

I guess I'm to blame for getting us involved. I'm the one who talked everyone into going to that first demonstration. Actually, I'm often the one who says, "Let's do this!" when I see something that piques my interest. The girls call these "Lauri's Adventures." Sometimes my adventures turn out to be a bust, sometimes they're a lot of fun, and sometimes they're difficult but transformative.

I was interested because the facilitators claimed this technique would help you get rid of old programs that no longer served you. I had plenty of those. I was also interested because I was ambitious. Anything that could help me succeed at my chosen career was something I wanted to check out.

Although we watched the woman at the demonstration go back to a painful part of her childhood, I was sure that this would not happen to me. I felt that I was coming to terms with my past and was making a good adjustment to new conditions. For instance, I was getting a divorce at the time, and yes, I did feel guilty about it, but I was comfortable with my decision. I held no grudges against my husband, who was a good man who always tried to do his best. He was the right person for me at the right time in my life. But that time had passed.

I was also working through the issues surrounding my strict religious background. I was raised a Lutheran, but that doesn't begin to show how deeply the church was embedded into my life. My mother was the secretary to the National Vice President of the Missouri Synod Lutheran Church, a very high position indeed. I attended a private Lutheran high school. My husband Gary and I met in a church activity group. His mother was also a secretary to a large Lutheran church in another suburb. Our families knew everybody who was anybody in the Lutheran church. I married my husband because I thought I had to—serious and passionate dating was supposed to lead to marriage, wasn't it?

Don't get me wrong. Lutherans are good people trying their best to live good and decent lives. It's true that they tend to be on the judgmental side, but the good they do far outweighs their judgments.

I believe in God and heaven. I treat others with love and respect. I pray. These attitudes are part of who I am. But I wasn't interested in bringing any of that up when I was using the technique. I was interested in improving my professional life and getting rid of habits that were holding me back from being successful.

At that first introduction, I volunteered to be one of the "guinea pigs." I had a "problem" picked out to work on. It was that no matter how much I got done, it never seemed to be enough. There was always more to do. I didn't want to be in frantic mode as much as I was. I wanted to feel satisfied with what I achieved.

I was good at following instructions, so I dutifully came up with a list of positive statements, and the facilitator muscle-tested me on each one. I must say I was surprised when my arm went down even though the statement wasn't the one I "thought" it would be. My primary statement turned out to be "I am good enough." Because my arm went down, that meant I was actually holding a belief that I was not good enough.

The facilitator asked me to remember a time when "I am good enough" was not true. To go back to the earliest time I could remember.

And into my mind popped—and pop is the right word, it was as if a memory just appeared like magic—my brother's birth, when I was three years old.

I was my parents' oldest child, and the apple of my dad's eye. He liked my mom to dress me up in pretty party dresses so he could take me on walks through the neighborhood and show me off. He thought I was special and beautiful. I thought he was the most wonderful man in the world.

Then when I was three, my brother Russ was born. My dad was ecstatic with his first son. It seemed like he was always holding the baby, and telling me that I had to be a good big sister. But what I remembered most was how sad I felt because I wasn't special to Dad anymore. I resented my brother for taking my dad away. Then I felt guilty because I loved my brother. How could I blame him, just an innocent little child? But I did. I wasn't a good big sister.

Then another memory popped in, from when I was a little older. I was ten and my brother was seven. He was on his first T-ball softball team. My father spent a lot of time with him, playing catch and teaching him baseball skills. They'd go out in the back yard and throw the ball around. I would stand at the window and watch.

The wave of emotion that passed through me as these images

arose was indescribable. How much I had loved my father, how much I missed him, jealousy and guilt over my much-loved brother. The result was that I lost it in front of everyone in that room. Huge sobs. Tears running down my face. Me—the one who was always in control! I was embarrassed, but it took me a long time to stop.

When I did, I felt a lot lighter. I was also able to see that I had completely internalized a message that my father never meant to send me—that I was not good enough. I believed I was second-best, and that no matter what I did, it was never going to be enough. I thought I had to prove to my father, and myself, that I was a good girl that I was good enough to be loved. I had drawn these wrong conclusions from my father simply showing his love for my brother. All through the years following, unknown to my conscious self, I had been operating on that belief of a three-year-old.

What an astonishing piece of self-knowledge that was. The events I recalled were not huge in themselves; after all, many children experience jealousy of new siblings. But the realization that my belief about those long-ago events could affect my life forty-some years later—now that was earth-shaking.

But the realization that my belief about those long-ago events could affect my life forty-some years later—now that was earth-shaking.

With the help of the facilitator, and the support of Barbara, Lee, Susan, Nicki and Gina, I worked out a new belief to replace the old one. I *was* good enough. Not just for my father, but for them. And for me.

Free: *Nicki*

The conference when we were first introduced to *The Enrichment Process*™ also happened to be the first conference I attended. I knew Barbara, but I had just that weekend met the other girls. I guess you could say I got to know everyone very well, very quickly. My relationship with them didn't start out in the shallow end, feeling each other out, sharing a few secrets, learning to trust, and all that. Instead I dived right into the deep end. The technique will do that to you.

I watched Lauri have her melt-down over her brother, and my love and admiration for her began at that moment. What a strong woman she was, and how committed to living a good life of service. Yet she didn't seem to realize how special she was, and it was that hidden lack of confidence that resonated with me. I knew that song. I'd sung it my whole life.

Watching Lauri gave me the courage to work on my own issues when we began the processing parties some months later. There were so many aha moments it's hard to pick just one. I did a session with Barbara as my facilitator about the turmoil I was in over losing my job and trying to start my own business. I know that without the insights I gained through that session my doubts about my ability would have overwhelmed me.

But this doesn't always have to be about those "big" issues. Probably the session that convinced me once and for all that this "woo woo" technique actually worked, and would work for me, was about something you could call trivial.

I had a problem with car sickness. If I was driving the car, I was fine, but if I was a passenger in the front or back seat, I'd get nauseous, and sometimes even have to throw up. It sounds like a silly problem, but it can actually affect your life. Years before, I was on a community softball team and sometimes we had to drive across town to our games, so we carpooled. I usually tried to be the driver, but one time someone else drove and we got stuck in rush-hour traffic. I was sitting in the middle of the back seat, squished between two women wearing their nice clean uniforms, and for over an hour I had to fight back spewing vomit. It seemed a lot longer than an hour.

I did some work about car sickness. I don't remember the exact words I used for statements, but I do remember the issue was about control. The memory that came up during the session was from when I was a teenager and was in a major car accident. The car I was riding in was rear-ended. I wasn't hurt, but the fact that there was nothing I could have done to prevent it from happening left me with a scared feeling of helplessness. The belief I internalized was that I wasn't safe if I wasn't in control.

After we did a session on this and I found a new belief to "tap into" (hah, that's a pun) I no longer experienced car sickness. It was that quick. Right after the session I didn't feel much different—no great "aaah" of relief or anything. But the next day I rode in my friend's car and it wasn't until we got to our destination that I realized I'd been chattering away happily all through the trip and never once even *thought* about getting sick. I've never been carsick since. I can sit in the passenger seat or the back seat; I can read a newspaper; I can read a map and navigate for the driver. I'm free!

Of course, not all sessions work that fast or have such obvious results. The most far-reaching work I did was with Lauri as my facilitator.

It was around 2000 when I decided to go back to school and get my college degree at last. I'm pretty sure I would never have attempted this without the support of the girls, but even with them, it was overwhelming. For one thing, I was old! I was 35, and in my world view at the time, 35-year-olds should be done with school by then. For another, school had always been hard for me, especially if I had to write anything. I was a terrible writer. I wrote in bullet points, like a business proposal. Just to think of being asked to write an essay with real sentences and paragraphs paralyzed me.

At one of our girls' weekends when it was only the six of us, I finally took the plunge and admitted what I thought none of them knew I felt—that I was a bad student, had always been a bad student, and was afraid I would always be a bad student. I asked them if they'd do a group process with me to change my belief. (The funny thing was I thought I had them all fooled, but I don't think they were surprised to hear that I had these insecurities.)

Lauri stepped right up and said she wanted to be the facilitator. She had been using the technique for years, as we all had, but always as the participant, never as the facilitator. "You'll be my first," she said, smiling all over her lovely face.

It was perfect that Lauri was my facilitator for this particular session. She had been an English teacher, her college degree was in English literature, and she was excited about awakening me to the beauty of language. Plus, we shared this special bond because both of us had issues with self-doubt, which we kept in our respective closets for years. I knew how crippling self-doubt could be, yet look what she had achieved! I admired Lauri as much as anyone I knew.

To be honest, I don't remember much about the session itself—what my primary statement was, what the memory I dug up was. One thing about using the technique is that it frees you to forget all those negative things you used to lug around with you. Once they're gone, they're really gone. What I do remember is Lauri's face when I "got it." It was simply shining with joy.

She told us afterwards that she was nervous about facilitating because it mattered so much that she did it right so that I got it. "I was focusing on the technique," she said, "trying to remember what came next and what I should say. But then all of a sudden my worry about the technique just went away. It wasn't about me anymore, it was all about Nicki. I just embraced her fears and her hopes, and they became my own. I hit a core. Goosebumps showed up all over my arms and hers. Everything just bubbled up."

That session was every bit as powerful for Lauri as it was for me, and it bonded us—and the other four who were witnessing—even more closely.

Lauri's support went a lot further than that one session. All through my educational journey, she was my mentor, especially when I needed to write something. I knew I could send it to her and she'd tell me what she thought. She was always supportive and positive. She never said, "Look, dumbass, you can't write like that!" That's what I would say to myself, but Lauri took my writing seriously. Pretty soon I was taking it seriously too.

Because of the magical technique and the support of Lauri and my other girlfriends, now I know I'm smart. (Plus, I don't throw up in the car!)

We have let go of a lot of stuff that most people carry around with them, so we are not weighed down. Our laughter is deep because there is nothing blocking it.

Lauri has been my primary mentor for my education, but our whole group has supported me. I think the big thing for me is that there is no judgment. None. This is important because *The Enrichment Process*™ makes you vulnerable. But we can be so comfortable with each other. When we laugh together—which we do all the time—we laugh deep belly laughs that come from where we really live. We have let go of a lot of stuff that most people carry around with them, so we are not weighed down. Our laughter is deep because there is nothing blocking it. We are light and we are free.

Pop! *Lee*

Most of the girls use this technique with their clients, but I don't because I'm not a coach. I facilitate training workshops and seminars where I stand up in front of the room and spout off. Like I've said, I love that limelight. *The Enrichment Process*™ is a much more intimate thing.

Still, I used this technique to get better professional results for myself. I remember one early session I did; my issue was that I wanted to do bigger conferences with large multi-national corporations. But I wasn't marketing to those people, and I didn't know why. What was stopping me?

I don't remember what my statements were, but through muscle testing we discovered that I had a negative experience with authority—my school—when I was twelve years old. Until that session, I had totally forgotten about it, but the belief I had internalized was that I couldn't hold my own with big organizations. No wonder I felt insecure about wanting to speak to IBM!

But the best part about this technique was not professional; it was personal. I loved our processing parties in the beginning when the six of us were just learning how to use the technique. We discovered so many things about ourselves and each other. We were eliminating old beliefs and replacing them with new ones every chance we got.

Later on, as we got better at using the technique, we tried variations. Sometimes one of us would be processed while the other five would act as group facilitators. Sometimes we'd pair up and do three processes at once, each pair in a different corner of the room, and then we would meet up and compare what we learned. Sometimes we would all work on one issue together, or sometimes one person might have a significant happening going on in her life and we all focused on her.

The trust we developed was unbelievable. You knew—and I

mean really knew—deep in your gut, that no one would make fun of you, break your confidence, or be anything but kind and loving. No one would judge you. Everyone would support you. Talk about freedom.

I think all women have the capacity to develop these kinds of bonds. They don't have to do it by using this technique. But I do think it made it easier and much, much faster.

One thing I like about this tool is that it has physical components like muscle testing and chest tapping. I've always been impatient with the "whys" of things. I want to know the "how." I don't have to know why it works, I just want to know that it does. *The Enrichment Process*™ gives you a "how" template. Even after being a professional speaker for 40 years, I sometimes get anxious before I get up to talk. But I discovered that if I tap my sternum before my speech and tell myself I'm a great speaker, it settles me down and brings me back to the present moment. I'm not worrying about what I'm *going* to say, I just focus on saying it.

When we first started learning how to do this work, I did have doubts that I was doing it "right." Lauri was overwhelmed with emotion, and Barbara would often do a process and say, "Oh my gosh, I felt that go right through my body and out my toes." But I never felt that, so I wondered if I was doing something wrong. Maybe I just didn't have what it takes to "get it." I didn't feel it working like the other girls did.

It took me a while to realize that it *was* working. Something would subtly shift in my life, and I would suddenly get that I didn't feel "that way" anymore. And I would remember doing a session about that issue months earlier. Everyone experiences the results differently. It doesn't seem to follow any sort of logic or conform to any psychological pattern. I've learned that it's best just to trust it and not bother asking questions about the "why."

Not only was I wrong in thinking my way wasn't the right way, I was wrong about never having an overwhelming emotional experience. Eventually I did have one that affected me powerfully, right through my body and out my toes.

———————▽———————

We were eliminating old beliefs and replacing them with new ones every chance we got.

Of course, being me, it had to have its humorous side. I wanted to do a process to help me change a minor annoyance, which was my fear of balloons, champagne corks, or anything else that might go "pop."

I know this sounds silly. Who ever heard of a grown woman being afraid of balloons?

It was the noise—or rather the anticipation of the noise—that got to me. If someone brought a balloon into a room, I'd get nervous. I'd start pacing. I'd move to the other side of the room. If I was invited to a child's birthday party, I'd ask if there would be balloons before I'd agree to come. Even if the party was for my own grandchild! ("Sorry, honey, Nana is afraid of balloons …") How embarrassing.

If I was out to dinner and someone ordered champagne, I would turn into a nervous wreck. I'd stick my fingers in my ears, close my eyes, and stay that way until the bottle was opened. Try explaining this at a business dinner—or worse, on a first date.

During muscle testing to find out what age I was when my

contrary belief occurred, it came out that I was only two. *Two?* My earliest conscious memories started when I was five. How could two be right?

And yet, as soon as I said the age out loud, a very old memory appeared in my mind. Just like that, there it was.

My older sister and I were standing outside our house, next to the side of the house where the coal bin was. My sister was seven, and I was two. She was mad at me for some reason. She was usually mad at me, mainly because people were always complimenting me on how cute I was, saying "Lee's the cute one," and ignoring my sister, who wasn't a pretty girl.

Suddenly my sister pushed me into the coal bin. It was dark in there except for the light coming in from the trap door I'd been pushed through. I saw my sister's face looking down at me and then "blam!" the trap door slammed shut with a huge bang and everything went totally dark.

As I remembered this experience, my whole body started to shake. I actually felt the terror rushing through me again, just as I had when I was two.

It took a while, but working with skilled questioning and muscle testing I was able to replace my old belief that sudden noises meant terror with a belief that I remained calm and safe no matter what.

As luck would have it, the day after this session we six girls were in the lobby of the hotel we were staying in, taking pictures of each other and generally horsing around, when a delivery man strode through the lobby with a balloon bouquet. All the other girls stopped and looked at me, waiting to see if I would hit the ground like I usually did.

But you know, I didn't even notice the balloons. I mean, I saw them, but they made no impression on me at all. I didn't even connect them to the session of the day before.

We make so many decisions about life and our place in it, and many of those decisions are based on faulty information. We tell ourselves stories with unhappy endings. We don't have to do that. As I've gotten older I have realized that many of my decisions were driven by my tremendous need to be heard, to be seen, to not be kept in the dark. I wanted to be let out of the coal bin.

Well, I've popped out now.

Fun is Fun: *Barbara*

It is typical for participants to have a memory from when they were very young suddenly jump into their conscious minds, seemingly from nowhere. But even though you know this, it's still a surprise when it happens to you. The balloon thing with Lee was huge. We were in a group of people that included not only the six of us, but other business associates as well. Lee was guarded about sharing outside our group; she knew how precious her professional image was, and how fragile.

So when I asked her, "Isn't there something you want to process on?" she said, "Oh, let's just do that silly balloon thing." She didn't want to share anything "big." She surely didn't expect what she got.

What she got was truly magic. Before she did that session, she used to be so jumpy. Any sudden noise would set her off; if someone slammed a door she'd jump out of her skin, usually upsetting a glass or a lamp or something. And if she even got a glimpse of a balloon I swear she started to twitch and stutter. But after that session, that stopped happening. She just looks at balloons with a sweet calm smile.

When I explain the technique, I tell people they don't have to take on the major skeletons in their closets; they can start with minor things, like Nicki did with getting sick in the car or Lee did with the balloons. I don't want to scare anyone off. But the truth is there are no minor things, really. The minor things are connected to the major things. They're all plot threads in the same story.

The important thing is not to be afraid of your own story. It's just a story that you told yourself. If the story is scary, you can tell yourself another one.

One of my early experiences was like Lee's—I thought it was a minor thing, and it was—but it was also connected to some major themes in my life.

I like to have fun. I'm always looking for ways to have fun. I've spent a lot of money on having fun. But often when I was in the middle of having fun, I'd suddenly feel an urgent need to wash the dishes or pay my bills. Every time I had a good time, I felt like I had to pay the price. It drove the girls crazy, because they were fond of having fun, too. So when I'd suddenly stop dancing and singing and begin sweeping the floor, they would get a little frustrated with me. I was frustrated with myself.

I said to one of the gals, "Let's do a session on this because this is irritating to not just be okay with the fact that I'm having fun."

The memory that surfaced was back when I was in seventh grade. I've always been a big sports person; I'm very physical and I like to move. Field hockey was my sport back then, and the coach was my gym teacher, Miss Nilles. She was a strict, no-nonsense person. I wasn't her favorite because I was also a great talker. I was one of those girls always chattering with my friends in the back while the teacher was trying to talk. I'm sure I was very annoying.

The important thing is not to be afraid of your own story. It's just a story that you told yourself. If the story is scary, you can tell yourself another one.

We'd be playing field hockey, and I was either right wing or left wing—far enough away from her that I felt safe to laugh and talk and not pay attention to the coach. But she'd catch me anyway and send me to detention. Seems like I was in detention a lot during seventh grade, almost always due to Miss Nilles. I hated detention, because it was one place you simply couldn't talk. You had to sit still and study. Every time I had fun I had to pay the price. That was the belief I took away from seventh grade.

During the session I replaced that belief with "I deserve to have fun," and the need to work while I was having fun stopped. What a relief—and not only just for me. My friends and family had more fun with me, too.

In subsequent sessions, though, other beliefs surfaced that were connected with that one. I had issues about having to choose between responsibility and fun, all with origins in my childhood and young adulthood.

My parents were divorced, which was unusual for when I was young in the 1950s, especially in the upper middle class suburbs where I was raised. My mom had a hard time with it; in those days, an attractive divorcee was viewed with suspicion. My sisters and I didn't see my dad much. He was a charming "party guy" who loved to have fun.

Instead, we were heavily influenced by my mother's parents, especially my grandfather. We spent every summer and holiday with them. I loved my grandfather. He was a successful Chicago architect and a man of strict moral standards and integrity; also a charitable, loving person who gave and gave and gave. He was wealthy, but he didn't flaunt it. During the Depression, with so many in the building trades out of work, he brought, at his own expense, workers to Michigan and put them to work building lake cottages that he designed. In the interior of the cottages, there is no molding. Everything meets and fits perfectly. My grandfather was an exacting and conscientious man. When he did something, he did it right.

The contrast between my two models of masculinity couldn't have been greater: my dad, who loved to laugh and have fun and didn't take care of us; and my grandfather, who worked hard and did. It doesn't take too much insight to see where I got my ideas about the relationship of fun and work. It has cropped up more than once in processing.

We can handle the truth. After all, we're the ones who get to define what the truth is.

Before I learned about *The Enrichment Process*™, I think I'd read every self-help book out there. All they did was frustrate me. They tell you to just think positive. But you can't do that if you're walking around with old programs that are holding you back. You can try and try, but all you do is create more stress, trying to be positive rather than getting rid of the old programs.

We are a story that we make up about ourselves. All the things we find in the programs are just pieces of the story. We grow up, we live in different places, we meet different people, and everything that we make up about ourselves is from those particular situations. But they are not necessarily the truth. They are our beliefs about the truth.

In the movie *A Few Good Men*, the Jack Nicholson character says, "You can't handle the truth." He was wrong. We can handle the truth. After all, we're the ones who get to define what the truth is.

In God's Hands: *Gina*

Knowing what I do now about my subconscious and how deep it can take you into yourself, it amazes me that I ever had the courage to do it. When we first learned about it, it sounded so outrageously kooky.

I was not an outrageous person, at least not outside the confines of my family. Although as a teenager in the seventies I wore my hair like Farrah Fawcett (don't blame me—we all did!), I was no Charlie's Angel leaping into danger at the first opportunity.

Up until I met Barbara and became a "bad girl," the most outrageous thing I ever did was go to Fort Lauderdale with a bunch of girlfriends during spring break my first year of college. One night we were in the Elbow Room, a bar which I believe is still there. It was a crazy place that catered to the college crowd with wet t-shirt contests and stuff like that. There must have been a hundred cute guys there. One of my girlfriends dared me to go up to one of them, start talking to him, and try to pick him up. She knew I'd never do it because this would be totally out of character for me. I just wasn't raised that way.

"There aren't any parents here," she said. "Go on, I dare you."

To her surprise, I said, "You're on," and walked to the other side of the room and started talking to this cute boy. Then I gave him a big hug and a kiss. Watching this, my girlfriends went crazy. They thought I had lost my mind.

What they didn't know was that boy I kissed was my cousin! I hadn't even known he was going to be in Fort Lauderdale that weekend, but when I spotted him across the room I knew I could win the dare. So I wasn't really being bold. I was just pretending.

Maybe I wasn't bold, but I could be boisterous, especially when I felt safe and protected within my family. Everyone in my family was loud; we certainly didn't repress much. Every emotion we felt was expressed. When my husband Guy and I were first dating, he told me he learned how my family worked by watching *The Sopranos*. "You've got everything but the guns," he said.

A lot of the sessions I did, especially in the beginning, dealt with my need to be safe and my fears of putting myself "out there." Even though I wanted out, my old programs kept pulling me back into the cocoon I was used to, where I was protected and safe. It has taken me 20 years of a variety of sessions to little by little peck my way out.

Yet, even now these issues come up. The difference is that now I know how to deal with them. One of my most satisfying experiences was when my husband, a firefighter who worked his way up through the ranks, was promoted to Chief. For the nearly 20 years before this, I never worried about Guy at work. I trusted that he would be safe even though his work took him into burning buildings. But when he became a chief, his jurisdiction changed and I was afraid for him.

The city of Chicago is not the safest place, and Guy was now going into some of its most dangerous neighborhoods, where there were drive-by shootings and gangs and innocent children killed. The killers don't care who they shoot; they might shoot at police officers—or firemen. Whenever Guy was working, I pictured him driving through these neighborhoods and someone shooting him dead, just because he was there.

I got so fearful that I started calling him every couple of hours, until he got me a police-and-fire scanner so I could listen to him while he was at work. I'd listen to him fighting the fire and communicating with the other firefighters. I couldn't go to sleep until I knew he was safe and returning to quarters.

Finally I asked the girls to do a session with me about this issue with Guy. It all went back to my fears about being safe. Even though by this time I was nearly fifty years old, there were still beliefs stuck in me from thirty years before.

The session allowed me to activate my faith around this issue. For me, faith is always where I go back to. My fear-based belief from the past was that no one was looking out for us, but my faith-based belief was that God would take care of Guy and me.

Sometimes people are looking for *The Enrichment Process*™ to bring them instantaneous relief, but that doesn't always happen. Big fireworks may not go off, your mouth may not fall open in shock, and you probably won't say, "I've learned the meaning of life!" Instead, later on something will happen that would usually trigger a fear-based response, and then you'll notice that you're handling it with grace, calm and peace.

Those are the qualities this technique awakened in me. I am more at peace—with myself, with the world outside. Even when there are crazy things going on in my life.

That's what the chest-tapping part of the session is for—to give us peace. We're actually tapping on our thymus gland, which is located underneath the breast bone, in the center of your chest. It's like burping a baby. You're trying to help the child be calm and peaceful, and get rid of things they don't need. That's exactly what this does. I don't need to get worked up. I have faith that I am okay.

I've always had faith, but working with the girls has made my faith deeper and stronger. I'm a practicing Catholic, although I think of myself as spiritual first, and Catholic second. I love the sacraments and rituals of the Catholic Church; they give me great comfort. But mostly I focus on what God wants for me. I accept that He is in control, not me. I know that I am safe because I'm always in God's hands.

Women Together: *Susan*

When I was in college in the seventies, I lived in an old two-story apartment building occupied mostly by single women. Down the hall lived a woman a little older than me who I respected a lot, because she was not only passionate about her politics, she lived them. She called herself an activist, a new term back then, and one that I wanted to have applied to me.

She started a Consciousness Raising Group for women in the building. Consciousness Raising Groups were all the rage within the budding women's movement at the time. We called ours simply CR; it made it seem more official. There were about ten of us who met every week. I felt immensely honored to be a part of CR, because the other women were so cool. We had an artist and several successful businesswomen. Everyone was forward-thinking and on fire to right the wrongs of the world, especially the wrongs against women.

To be honest, much of the time we ended up talking about our love lives and men. We weren't hardcore feminists, but we had fun, and we developed a deep bond that was based on our common vulnerability and the courage to be open about our deepest fears and desires. That was the beginning of my recognition of the power of women coming together in groups to support each other.

We weren't hardcore feminists, but we had fun, and we developed a deep bond that was based on our common vulnerability and the courage to be open about our deepest fears and desires.

When my mom got sick, it was the experience with CR that gave me the idea to form a support group for women with breast cancer. I invited therapists, nurses, and other professional women to come together and talk about the issues that breast cancer patients faced. Even though my mom died and the group floundered later, what I took from the experience was that groups of women had the power to transform the lives of each woman in the group—and anyone else who came in contact with them.

I stored these experiences in the back of my mind somewhere. I was in my early twenties then, but it wasn't until I was nearly forty that I became part of another transformative group of women—the "Bad Girls," as we laughingly came to call ourselves. Maybe we jelled so well and so fast because some of us already knew that a group of women could be powerful, but it was also due to learning *The Enrichment Process*™ techniques. Due to this work, our coming together was not only fast, it was deep.

We were all so into it, and so comfortable with each other that we'd just call up and say, "Hey, I need a session. Let's all get together." It wasn't long before we were adding special "girls' weekends" as well.

After we worked with the technique, we'd all feel so light, as if heavy burdens had fallen off our shoulders. We were totally energized, ready to embrace whatever came our way next.

This was especially true when the issues we uncovered during processing were traumatic or painful. Everything came up in our processing parties. I had many beliefs that originated from my history with my father. My dad went to war when he was only 17, which made him a tough-ass kind of person. Even though he was young, he advanced through the ranks and was in charge of a battalion on the front lines of combat. He often had to decide who lived and who died. This meant that as a father he had little sympathy for skinned knees or broken hearts. Not to mention any kind of back talk.

He pretty much ran our family, and no one stood up to him

without consequences, not even my mom. The belief that I took from watching them together was that marriage was hurtful for women. That belief came up in a lot of sessions.

It's true that after doing a session, you often forget the experience and the process itself. This is because processing frees you from having to remember; you've dealt with the memory and the story you told yourself about it, and replaced it with a new one. But one session I vaguely remember brought up an incident when I was around sixteen. My dad had been mean to me, and I seriously considered running away. I wanted so much to get away from him.

My facilitator—I think it was Barbara—said, "What did you need to know then? If you look at little Susie when she was 17 years old, what did you need to know about yourself then? What did you need to know about the world?"

I said, "I need to know that I'm going to be okay. I need to know that I'm powerful and strong and I'll grow up. I need to know that he's operating out of fear, not love. He's small, and I'm bigger."

Barbara said, "Now think of a time in the future, maybe some event coming up, when you want to take that knowledge with you. What would it look like, and what would you be doing?"

"I know I have to go in and speak to a CEO of a company who kind of looks like my dad," I said. "He's in the position of authority in the meeting I have to attend next week. What I need to take with me is the knowledge that I'm powerful. I need to take with me the feeling that I'm wise. I need to take with me the confidence that I can speak up and be heard and acknowledged for the expert I am."

Then while tapping my chest I imagined the meeting, using all the sensory details I could think of and feeling all the emotions I could, from that place of confidence and wisdom. Incidentally, the meeting the following week went great.

When you are a witness to someone going back into their deepest childhood pain point, and hear them talk about what they needed to know then as a child, it activates such a feeling of love and protection. You can see the childlike innocence and goodness that still resides at their core, and you so want them to have what they need.

We all have held certain beliefs at some point in our lives. It's just human. *I'm not good enough. I'm not worthy. There's something wrong with me.* If life was perfect, if we had perfect (that is, not human) parents and caregivers, then maybe we would have been taught how to tell ourselves better stories. But life isn't perfect, and our parents are human beings with parents of their own, and we all just need to forgive each other. And learn to tell ourselves better stories *now*.

When we were working with each other we absolutely saw the good in each other. We saw our strengths and our power; we saw our innocence and our trust; we saw into the essence of who we were as human beings.

As a result, we wanted the best for each other; we wanted it with the force and depth of a parent's hopes for her children. Regardless of what the individual issues were, we hoped that we all would be blessed with light and love, power and strength.

It's like we saw the god in each other. This was the same with every single session we did, every single time.

Yet the technology remains just a means to an end. It's a powerful technique, but it's not the end. The end is the bond that we six women formed, made of honesty and openness, courage and vulnerability, support and commitment to each other. And absolute, total acceptance.

I sensed when I was young that women in groups were powerful. Now I know that I was right.

The Buena Vista Strut: Dreams Do Come True

FOUR

Angels Shout If You Don't Pay Attention When They Whisper

*M*aybe the depth of connection we experienced doing processing was what made us such a strong unit so fast, but don't get the wrong idea—processing was only one of our rituals that developed. There is so much more to us than using the technique.

Maybe it was the great places we went on our "girls' weekends." Many of the early conferences were in Florida, so we'd schedule a girls' weekend at the end of the conferences. Perhaps that tropical weather loosened us up even more. After all, four of us lived around Chicago. Susan lived in Pennsylvania; it was only Lee in Florida who could laze around palm trees whenever she wanted—not that Lee ever lazed anywhere. Lee had too much zing. Her house, where we had girls' weekends for the first five years or so, was in a community called Wildcat Run—what an appropriate name that was. We all turned into wildcats as soon as we got there. It was right on a golf course with a huge swimming pool and a hot tub connected to the pool. The hot tub often turned brown when we were there because we had a habit of drinking White Russian cocktails while we soaked. (And spilled, and laughed, and spilled some more.) Then when Lee wanted to downsize, Barbara and her husband, Rick, bought the Wildcat house as a second home, so we had two places to go in Florida. But then we branched out; over the years we've gone to Susan's beach house on the Jersey shore, and of course exotic vacations like Bahamian cruises and Club Med in Florida. Okay, it wasn't the places we went either.

Was it the other ongoing rituals we did, no matter where we were? We always had great food and we always and we mean *always*—found time to make our special martinis. We always found time and places to sing and dance—sometimes even in public, God help us all. But more often we were by ourselves. Someone would always bring music, usually Gina, and with Gina that meant The Carpenters. When Gina was a teenager, she wanted to *be* Karen Carpenter. But someone else would bring Stevie Wonder or Springsteen, and there we'd be, dressed in PJs, sweats, or dirty socks, swiveling our hips to *Glory Days* or warbling *We've Only Just Begun* with a martini in one hand. Some of us even went without make up and didn't comb our hair, although that never applied to Lee, who always manages to look perfect. The rest of us have given up trying to figure out how she does it. Maybe she was born with mascara on her eyelashes.

And oh, our angel cards! They have been a part of every girls' weekend from the very beginning. None of us can remember now who brought them to the first weekend; maybe they brought themselves.

Many people treat divination cards as just a party game, but if you do them with intention, they are much more. We use

Angel Cards by Doreen Virtue, which are illustrated with beautiful paintings of angels on one side, and a message or an answer just for you on the other. They come with a guidebook that helps you divine the meaning of the cards that you choose.

We don't have a set practice for using Angel cards. Sometimes after we've been together for a couple of hours, we'll spread the cards out face down in a big circle and each of us will choose a card by holding our hand over the card until we feel the energy of one card draw our hand down. The amazing thing is the cards we draw are always—and again, we mean *always*—specific to whatever it was we were talking about. We're used to it by now, but at first it made our mouths drop open. Then we talk about the cards we drew. We probe into the meaning they have for us.

Or sometimes we'll start each morning of our girls' weekend with the angel cards which drops us into such deep sharing that we stay there all day.

Or sometimes we'll ask, out loud or silently, specific questions about an issue that may be coming up. Or someone might just want to ask, "What do I need to know about today?"

Whichever way we use the Angel cards, they connect us fast and deep to each other. And to our angels, of course.

But we're practical businesswomen, so it's not all angel cards and processing, or even White Russian cocktails and palm trees. We're in the same industry, we all own our own businesses, we're all ambitious and successful—so of course we talk about business. In our everyday lives, we go out into the world and teach training programs to help people understand each other better, and connect better with the corporations that employ them. When we get together we restore ourselves so we can go back out into the world and do that kind of work again. We throw ideas around. We discuss particular challenges and how each of us might handle them. We applaud our successes and try to glean the lessons from any mistakes. Each one of us makes the others better at what we do.

One of the things unique about the six of us is that we share a profession. Training and coaching is all about helping others ask questions and probe for the truth. But you can't just limit that to business, can you?

So finally, just like in Susan's CR group in the 1970s, we talk about our romantic relationships. We are women, and that's what women do. We've seen each other go from single to married, from married to single, some of us more than once. When we first met, all of us were in transition from one state to another, and that too deepened our connection.

When you really know another person, when you witness who they are at their most vulnerable core, you can become that person's angel guide yourself. In other cultures and other times, marriages were arranged by the parents of the bride and groom. Part of the reason for that was economic ownership, sure, but another part was because the parents loved their children, and knew that they might not know enough about the world—or about themselves—to make wise choices. In a funny way, that's what we Bad Girls do for each other in our relationships. We help each other make wiser choices through our transitions, by supporting each other while we let go of bad relationships, and nudging each other to recognize the good ones.

One thing about transition—it never really stops. We are always in transition. That's why we will always need each other. And that's why we keep on doing our little rituals that make us real.

So it wasn't just one thing that brought and kept us together. It was all of them: processing, angel cards, singing and dancing, helping each other succeed at business and at love, openness, vulnerability, and the courage to share. *The Enrichment Process*™ gave us insights into our history and our psychological needs. The angel cards brought us into connection with Spirit. The sharing about our relationships opened our hearts to each other. And the singing and dancing anchored us in our bodies, bringing it all into physical reality. These practices made it possible for us to come together and navigate the waters of transition in ways that we could never have done by ourselves.

And yet we just call them our "girls' weekends." What an understatement.

That Law of Attraction: *Barbara*

When the Bad Girls first jelled, I was in relationship limbo, in transition just like the others. I'd recently separated from my nightmare second husband, who I married because he was one of those charming fun guys who up to then was one of my two standard choices in men.

I was often attracted to these charming types who churned my insides to butter, used me up, and left me empty and scared. Yes, just like my own father. In fact, my second husband even looked like my father. After being burned, I'd veer wildly the other way, toward the responsible, take-care-of-business type who was safe but had difficulty communicating what was in his heart. Leaving me—guess what—empty and scared.

I was so tired of this father/grandfather seesaw, a helpless prey to my own attractions. I wanted to control what and who I was attracted to. It wasn't until I was introduced to *The Enrichment Process*™ and the Law of Attraction—that what you focus on appears—that I thought I might have a chance of attracting someone both responsible *and* fun.

And if I forgot, I had five strong women gently reminding me. At our girls' weekends, I did many processes about who I wanted to attract, and the kind of man I deserved to have in my life. I described him to the girls as if he already existed in my life. He was good looking, with an impish smile and eyes that twinkled. He could make me laugh, and he liked to laugh. But he had a serious side, too; he was interested in how he could contribute to the betterment of the world, corny as that sounds. He was adventurous, not held back by fear. He loved my friends and my children. My sons liked him. He had good relationships with his own family. He could communicate his feelings; he wasn't emotionally constipated. Oh, I was very detailed.

Still, I wasn't actively "looking." I was learning to put what I wanted out there, and believe that whatever was best for me would happen. I dated some, but if there was no one special for a while, I mostly just shrugged.

To be honest, I wasn't totally successful with my new "let go and let God" attitude. As a year went by, and then two, I began to think that the Universe had something else in store for me. I tried not to be disappointed. But I was.

Yet when we did the angel cards, they nearly always were some variation of the message: "He's coming. Be patient." Once I consulted a psychic, and she told me the same thing.

"You're going to meet the most amazing man, and have the most exciting life," said the psychic.

"Really?" I said. "When?"

"In about two years."

"I can't wait," I moaned. Patience had never been my strong suit.

"He's worth waiting for," she said.

So I sighed and said okay, I'll wait. I focused on building my business and raising my kids. And I had fun with my girlfriends. I mean, who says you have to have a man around to have fun?

About two years after the psychic said I would, I met him. His name is Rick and he *is* the most amazing man. He has every one of the attributes I had been focusing on. Every one.

But I hadn't listed impulsive, and Rick certainly isn't.

He is patient, which is exactly the quality I had been focusing on, trying to learn it myself. The Universe sent me the teacher I ordered. That damn Law of Attraction again.

I recognized him as "the one" the first time I met him. I just knew, don't ask me how. We went out once, and I wondered (not aloud, thank God) if he would want a big wedding. We went out again, and I thought how handsome he would be when he was ninety. On the third date, he kissed me for the first time—only he didn't kiss me on the lips, he kissed my neck, oh so casually. My knees buckled anyway. I thought, "I'm gone." And I was.

On the fourth date, we got intimate and I was sure that he felt the same way about me. I couldn't be mistaken. But he didn't say so. He just looked so.

I was talking to Lauri the next day, and she said, as girlfriends do, "So? What happened on your date? Did you sleep with him?"

When I said yeah, I did, she said, "Oh my God! I've got to meet him!" and demanded to do so that very evening. We went out for drinks. Afterwards, she told me, "You were right. He's the one."

But it wasn't that simple. As I said, Rick is not impulsive. He is honest and straightforward and full of integrity, and his word is of vital importance to him. What he says he means. He doesn't make commitments he can't keep. He doesn't use words like "love" lightly—not unless he means it for the rest of his life.

He told me this on our first date, so it's not like I didn't know. But I was so in love with him that I figured he would make an exception for me.

Well, he didn't. He made me wait until he was absolutely sure. We dated for three years before I heard those words *I love you*. He had taken me out to dinner at our favorite restaurant, and just like in the romantic movies he handed me a little jeweler's box right after we got our drinks. In it was a heart-shaped locket. Engraved inside the locket was *I love you*.

I'm glad now that he made me wait to hear it. Because I have never since doubted that he meant what he said. I know in the deepest part of my being that I am loved by this amazing man.

At the same time I'm grateful that the girls were there to prop me up during those three years, or I might have gone nuts waiting for him. Every time I despaired of ever hearing him say I love you, they reminded me of the ways he showed that he loved me. They knew, even when I had forgotten, that he was the right one for me. He was just a tad slow!

Rick loves my friends. Not just each of them individually, but he loves the idea of them as a group. We make him laugh. He thinks we are a scream, and really, he's quite right. We are a scream.

But he knows we get what we want, and he recognizes our power. He also gets the Law of Attraction. Our mastery of this law has benefitted him directly. We danced him right into a new house.

It was several years after we got married (oh yes, we got married—after he said, "I love you" he sped up a lot) when Rick and I wanted to buy another home. We already had one vacation home in Florida, which we purchased from Lee, but then we saw another house that we both wanted. It was beautiful, perfect, and cost way more than we wanted to pay.

The house had a name: Buena Vista. I cut out a picture of Buena Vista from a real estate magazine, made six copies, and at a girls' weekend I handed them out to the girls.

"This is the house I want," I said. "Can you help me get it?"

We did a process on it. We did Angel cards. Each of us pasted a picture of Buena Vista into our day timers, where we'd see it every day. Across the picture I wrote, "My house." The other girls wrote, "Rick and Barbara's house." If someone happened to catch a glimpse of the picture in my day timer, they'd often say something like, "Wow! Is that your house?" And I'd respond, "Not yet, but it's going to be."

We didn't focus on how we were going to purchase a house we couldn't afford. That's not how the Law of Attraction works. We just focused on the house itself, and left it up to the Universe to lead us to the how.

At the following girls' weekend a couple of months later, which happened to be in my house in Florida, we made it even more real. Dancing, or any physical activity, is a great way of making things that aren't real yet, become real. We did the Buena Vista Strut.

Remember the strut that John Travolta made famous in *Saturday Night Fever*? The Buena Vista Strut is kind of like that, only more elegant and with martinis.

We started strutting around the living room while we were having our cocktails, chanting "Buena Vista, Buena Vista, we live at Buena Vista" and trying not to spill the drinks. We held our photos of Buena Vista in front of us and pretended we were strutting over the bridge to the Jacuzzi we saw in the photo. As we followed each other in a kind of conga line around the room, we were laughing so hard the chanting almost stopped. But as we drank the rest of the martinis, faint cries of "Buena Vista!" could be heard.

Rick loves this story. He says he wishes he could have been there. We're all kind of glad he wasn't.

Rick and I moved into Buena Vista the following year. The Law of Attraction is real. Don't let anyone tell you it isn't.

You Get What You Need: *Gina*

I get teased a lot because I love The Carpenters. I can't help it. Their lyrics are upbeat, the melodies are soothing, and okay, the songs remind me of my youth. And although the girls like to make fun of me, I've noticed that they know all the words to any Carpenters song I care to sing. We even have a video of us using an upturned empty wine bottle as a microphone and singing *We've Only Just Begun* into it. Everyone's lips are moving, not just mine.

I love our girls' weekends. We get to be as silly as we want, and we usually want. Fun is a big part of them, but they're work, too, of a sort. We work on ourselves; it's the kind of work that makes you feel you've really accomplished something. Processing, angel cards, and just sitting around bearing our hearts to one another may not sound like work, but that's because we've told ourselves the wrong stories about what work really means. Work is a good thing. Work can be fun.

We work on ourselves; it's the kind of work that makes you feel you've really accomplished something.

One of our commonalities in the beginning was that we were all in some kind of relationship transition. Nearly all of our current partners came into our lives after we started having girls' weekends, and I don't think it's a coincidence that these significant others are the ones who were "it." I think it's because we had each other to bounce our thoughts and feelings, fears and desires, against. In return we got honest and loving feedback from people who really knew us, right down to our toes, as Barbara would say. This meant we didn't make as many stupid mistakes as we'd made in the past.

I had been married once before, for a couple of years in my early twenties. I think I got married because I wanted to be independent from my family so I wouldn't have to be so responsible. I chose a wild young man who I thought could show me how to do this. He did, too. He enjoyed sowing his wild oats in every field he could find, and I found out I didn't like the irresponsible life after all.

By the time I met the Bad Girls, I had been single for nearly ten years. I liked being single and enjoyed the dating game, but I sensed that I was ready for something more. When I was young I didn't know what I wanted in a relationship, only what I didn't want. While I was just dating, I didn't bother to think about what I wanted in a man. But this time, working with the girls on the Law of Attraction, I got specific and positive.

It's not that I was picky, exactly, but I was in my early thirties and I didn't want to waste any more time kissing frogs. I knew I wanted someone solid, conservative and responsible. I wanted a godly man; he didn't have to be Catholic like me, although it would be nice. The biggest factor was that he had to be a family-oriented person. If he didn't get what family was all about, he would never make it in mine—my big Italian bunch who kissed everyone upon arrival and kissed them again upon departure, that all-encompassing *Soprano* kind of thing. If he couldn't manage that and some people can't—then he was out.

And I wanted someone who wanted to try to have kids. I wasn't sure I could have them, but at least I wanted to try.

So that's what I put out there. And I'm sure you can guess what I'm about to tell you next—I found him. He was exactly what I'd ordered, almost like he had been planted in my life. Which he had been; *I* planted him.

I met Guy at one of my best friend's weddings. She and I had been friends since grammar school. Guy was a good friend of one of my other friend's husband; they were both firemen. I had heard about Guy, but had never met him.

At the reception, I was hanging out with a bunch of my old

girlfriends and they were talking about him. "Guy is perfect for you, Gina," said Terri and Sheryl, and everyone else echoed, "Yeah." I wasn't buying it, though. I kept saying, "Oh come on, stop it. I hate it when you do this." All my married friends were always trying to fix me up. I'd heard this song before.

Then someone pointed him out to me, standing across the room. And I swear to God, my knees buckled. I couldn't breathe. It was total physical overload. I even said out loud, "That's it. Stick a fork in me, I'm done."

My girlfriends' eyes lit up. They started pestering me to go over and talk to him. This wasn't new behavior for them; they were always trying to get me to go up and talk to strange men. The only time they'd ever succeeded was in Fort Lauderdale when I'd fooled them with my cousin. It just wasn't me; I didn't do stuff like that.

Except this time. I put down my drink, took a deep breath, and walked right up to Guy and asked him to dance.

"No, thank you," he said politely.

I felt all of the air leak out of my body. My face felt as though it would slither off my bones. Somehow I managed to walk back across the room. I went straight up to the bar and ordered a cocktail. Then I drank it down in one gulp.

What I didn't know was Guy had already noticed me, when I'd read the blessing for the bride at the wedding, and thought I was pretty cute. But he also noticed that I'd come with a date. The "date" was just a friend, but he didn't know that.

After he turned me down for a dance, his friend Steve, who knew me, whacked him on the arm and demanded, "What's wrong with you? She's got looks, she cooks, and she's got a big fat checkbook." Who knew Steve could be so poetic?

Well, as I was drinking whiskey and mortification at the bar, friends were explaining to Guy that my date was not really a date, and besides, he'd already left, and other friends were trying to get me to go up and ask Guy to dance again. I said there was no way I would ever ask a man to dance again, and then somehow I found myself calmly walking across the room and up to him again. "Dance?" I said. And this time he said okay.

And so it began. By the following month I was ready to get married. I knew he was the one. All my friends knew he was the one.

But we didn't get married until nearly three years later.

Sounds familiar, doesn't it? My relationship with Guy began just about the same time as Rick and Barbara started dating. Just like Rick, Guy had these rules about knowing *for sure* the relationship could last forever, before you actually committed to anything. Guy called it his two-year rule.

Okay, I know this is a responsible position, and I had specifically asked for a responsible man, but my God…two years? Sometimes I wanted to hit him. I wanted to get married. I wanted to marry him. I wanted to have a baby—his baby. Didn't he realize how *old* I was?

I am so glad I had Barbara around to talk with during these years, because she was going through the same stuff with Rick. It's pretty funny to think back to what we told each other. Every time she complained about Rick making her wait, I'd remind her of his integrity and how she could totally trust him. When I moaned about how Guy didn't seem to understand that I needed to get married now, Barbara would talk about how responsible Guy was, how committed to his family, how he always tried to do right.

"We'll just have to wait it out, sister," she said, whenever she wasn't complaining about having to wait it out herself. Then I'd say it back to her.

I was 35 when we got married. I've got to laugh—one of my biggest issues was safety, and I married a fireman, not exactly the safest profession you could ask for. God always gives you opportunities to learn. I'd been doing all these processes on my safety issues, and so I was sent a fireman to fall in love with. God has such a sense of humor.

His next lesson wasn't quite as funny. Guy and I tried to get pregnant right away, which was a courageous decision. It wasn't just because I was in my mid-thirties; I had also been told by various doctors that because of some earlier problems I might not be able to get pregnant. Even if I was able to conceive, I might not be able to carry a child to term. I was burdened with many fears. In marrying Guy, I had become a "Bonus Mom" to his son, Jimmy. I thought, if we didn't get pregnant, could I be satisfied with not having a child of my own?

It took a few years of regular disappointments, but eventually I did become pregnant. You might think that this success made me the proverbial glowing mother-to-be, but I wasn't. Maybe because of the fears I had, but also because I was so sick. For nine straight months, I barfed all day long. My feet and hands swelled until they felt as if they would pop. I was always tired. I didn't feel like planning for the baby, I just wanted to go to sleep and stay that way. On top of this, I felt so guilty. A good mother wouldn't feel this way, would she? I was terrified to let anyone know how unhappy and scared I was.

About my sixth month, we got together for a girls' weekend in Chicago. When I arrived, I literally ran into the room shouting, "I need a process!"

It took enormous courage for me to admit that I hated being pregnant. I felt like I'd been flayed open and my most vulnerable parts exposed. I was so ashamed, so guilty, so scared. Yet somehow, I knew that Lauri, Susan, Nicki, Lee, and Barbara would be able to heal me.

It all poured out. "I'm scared out of my mind to be a parent. I'm afraid that I'm transmitting this bad energy to my little baby inside me. Am I crazy? Am I just selfish? Don't I love my baby enough? I just want this to be over. I shouldn't feel this way. Help me make sense of this or I'm going to burst."

There is nothing more healing than to have someone listen to—and really hear—your deepest vulnerabilities, the things that make you cringe and shake with shame and fear, and have that person love you completely with no trace of judgment. When there are five people surrounding you with this energy, you *know* you will be alright. I have learned since then that my experience is not unusual. We have been told a story that every woman's pregnancy is a golden time. But the truth is that every woman's pregnancy is unique to her. I could tell myself that I was a bad mommy because pregnancy was difficult for me, or I could tell myself that I was a good mommy because I undertook something difficult because I wanted my son so much. It's really up to me which story I believe.

One thing I've learned is that once you get what you want, you don't get to stop there. There's always more coming. Once I became a mother, then I started to work on my fears that I wouldn't be a good one.

I go to my girlfriends for help there, too. They know I am a good mom. I know it, too, in my heart, but it's good to be reminded. Even today, this issue crops up from time to time, as my son grows and turns from a child into a man. What will it be like to be the mom of a teenage boy? Will I be able to handle it?

There is nothing more healing than to have someone listen to—and really hear—your deepest vulnerabilities, the things that make you cringe and shake with shame and fear, and have that person love you completely with no trace of judgment.

Good thing I've got the right tools to answer those questions—processing, angel cards, and five supportive women friends. Not too long ago I volunteered to take four 12-year-old boys—my son and three of his friends—on a camping trip in a 28-foot RV. "I must have lost my mind," I whined to the girls, during a girls' weekend shortly before the camping trip. "What am I going to do with four 12-year-old boys for five whole days? I know I'm gonna lose it." Anyone who has spent any time at all with pre-adolescent males will understand my nervousness. They have a lot of energy. I mean a lot.

"Let's pull an angel card," suggested Susan. "It'll rest your mind."

She was right. I pulled the Nature card. The message of the card was something like, "Become one with Nature. Appreciate its beauty." My focus immediately shifted. The trip wasn't about *me* dealing with boys. It was about *us* experiencing nature and learning to appreciate it.

It turned out to be a great trip. Everyone learned something. The boys were boys, full of noise and enthusiasm. I stayed calm.

I hold a special place within the Bad Girls. The others are either childless or their children are grown. I'm the only one raising a child right now. Sometimes I can't do all the things they do, or join them for their trips, because my family must come first. That's okay with all of us. No, it's more than okay—it's right. I think I'm the special Mom project for everyone. My son has become everyone's son.

My goal is to always be in alignment with God. My girlfriends help me do that. Just by their presence, they remind me that if it's for the highest good, God will always give me exactly what I need.

How YOU Doin'? *Nicki*

God, our girls' weekends—where do I start? Every time we get together, something big happens. Even if we don't recognize it as big right then.

One such momentous weekend we spent at a Lake Michigan-cottage. For some reason, that was a time most of us seemed to be both beginning and ending something. And boy did we need to talk about it.

It was an unseasonably cold spring that year, and on the shores of Lake Michigan it was even colder. The cottage's only heat came sporadically from an archaic baseboard heating system and a wood-burning fireplace that heated the front room sort of, and the other rooms not at all.

That first night we huddled around the fireplace, playing "How YOU Doin'?" This is said Italian-style, like that guy on *Friends*. Either Gina or I will start it, because I admit, sometimes we play up the Italian part. We're the only ones who can say it right; the rest of the girls try, but they just can't. To see and hear six-foot, slender, blonde Lee trying to say "how you doin?" like an Italian is an absolute scream.

But however funny "How YOU Doin" sounds, it's a real way to check in with each other. After dinner we made our martinis—someone else will have to tell about the martinis, because I'm still learning—and we took turns telling each other how we were doin' in between dancing around the room. It was midnight before anyone remembered to call home and let them know we got there okay.

We blame Rick for what we did next. Barbara called him to say goodnight, and while she was on the phone she suddenly started laughing so hard her martini came out her nose. "He says we don't have a hair on our ass if we don't go skinny dipping in the lake," she snorted.

Those martinis warm you up pretty good (or maybe it was the dancing), because this idea struck us as a good one even though the thermometer outside registered 31 degrees. "Let's go!" someone said, and the next thing I knew we were running down the hill toward the lake, shedding clothes as we went. We plunged into that cold black lake and stayed there a grand total of probably three seconds. Then we ran back up the hill and burst into the cabin again, making straight for the fire. We were still laughing, but I'm pretty sure all of us were sober by then.

I had to get permission from the girls to write about this, because that story was covered by a spit-pact swear. When I was little, my sister and I had spit-pact swears about things we didn't want anyone else to know. We'd lick our thumbs, touch each other's thumb, lick our own thumbs again, and swear not to tell. Actually my sister and I still do this today sometimes, and now so do the Bad Girls. Spit-pact swears mean you can't even tell your significant other, unless you have permission from the whole group.

So when we were standing there shivering and dripping, someone called out, "spit-pact!" But now we think it's just too good a story not to share and besides, it's not like anyone saw us—it was completely dark out there!

The next morning it was even more frigid in the cabin, so we made a fire in the fireplace, and still in our PJs (actually, I was wearing Joe Boxer flannel pants and a bright orange Saugatauk sweatshirt, and the others were similarly elegant), set up six chairs in a semi-circle facing the fire and started to talk.

It was still cold, but that didn't stop us from talking. Periodically one of us, usually me or Gina, would throw a coat on and streak outside to get more wood to put on the fire. The room got warmer. It also got smokier. We'd been talking for over two hours before we noticed that we had been coughing and waving our hands in front of our faces for nearly that whole time. Finally Susan said, "Um, is it really smoky in here, or is it just me?"

We forgot to open the flue. And we were so involved in each other that we just kept pushing the smoke away, with our minds as well as our hands.

We had to open the door and windows to let the smoke out (and the cold back in). But after the smoke cleared, we went back to our semi-circle, still wearing our sweats, PJs, and wooly socks. We drank coffee, talked, ate breakfast, talked, ate lunch, talked, ate snacks, talked…and finally around five o'clock in the afternoon we got dressed. The only time anyone got up was to get some food, which we'd bring back to the front room to share while we talked. No way was anyone going to miss anything.

You might wonder what we were talking about that was so engrossing that we ignored everything else, even a smoke-filled room.

We were fascinated with each others' lives. Big things were happening!

Lee announced that she had decided to divorce her third husband. We all knew this was the right step for her, and were so glad she had come to this conclusion, too. We also knew it was going to be a tough journey for her, financially and emotionally. We did a process around her fears and how she wanted to handle the upcoming changes.

Then Lauri shared that she, too, had made a huge decision about her current relationship. She had been dating a man who we all had reservations about. He had a tendency to use putdowns, especially with her, and none of us liked it. Of course we supported her no matter what, but we were delighted when she told us she was giving him back the huge honking diamond ring he had given her, and breaking it off.

Susan had just started dating, only she insisted it wasn't dating and that they were just friends. He was perfect for her, but she claimed he wasn't her type, and besides they were business colleagues. She did admit he was kind, and witty, and fun to be with. Oh, and hard-working, educated, generous, a man of integrity. And did she mention he had spiritual depth and was a fascinating conversationalist? But not her type. Nope. We just listened to her, and hoped she would start listening to herself soon.

Barbara and Gina were in committed relationships, so then it was my turn. When I first met the girls, I was going through the finale of a ten-year relationship, and since it had ended I'd been determinedly single—although the girls were always on the lookout for possible partners for me. So far they hadn't found any, which was fine with me. Lauri had offered to write my personality description for a dating service, however, I hadn't been in a hurry. I figured when it happened, it happened. And in the meantime, I was having fun and learning about myself.

So when the girls asked me stuff like, "How YOU Doin?" I said I was "doin" great, and loved being single. It was a good time in my life to get in touch with who I was and what I wanted, and who better to share this realization with than my Bad Girls!

Opening My Heart: *Susan*

Moving to Chicago was a turning point in my life. It was there that I met Lauri, then Barbara and Lee, then Gina and Nicki. I also dumped the guy I moved to Chicago for, and almost immediately took up with another man, who I unfortunately married. All this was happening about the same time.

Everyone in your life is there to teach you something, or you are in their life to teach them. But usually you don't meet so many teachers all at once; no wonder my head was spinning! I used to think it a shame that I didn't meet the girls long before I met my first husband, because if I had I'm sure I never would have married him. One penetrating look from Barbara accompanied by the question, "What are you doing?" would have made me pause, at least.

But today I know better. I needed to marry him. Maybe I could have learned what that experience taught me in another way, one a little less painful, but I bet I wouldn't have learned it so well or so fast.

Everyone in your life is there to teach you something, or you are in their life to teach them. But usually you don't meet so many teachers all at once . . .

When I first met him, he was charming, attractive, and funny. He paid attention to me. He courted me. He was all those things right up until the honeymoon.

On the honeymoon I wanted to throw my ring away. I knew I had made a mistake. He was a control freak, and verbally and physically abusive if he felt I was out of his control. He drank too much, showing all the signs of an alcoholic—which I had totally missed until we got married. To be fair to myself, he had hidden those signs very well. It wasn't until we got married and he felt he "had me" that he let his real self emerge.

He kept me off-balance, because I never knew at what point he was going to go ballistic. He'd throw things. He'd threaten to kill me. I lived in a perpetual state of fear. You always hear, "Why do people stay?" I never got it until it was me. Then I understood too well.

There were times when he was fine, and his better angels would shine forth, calling me to love him in spite of my fear. Part of me did love him. I wanted it to work. We went back and forth, back and forth; we probably went to at least ten marriage counselors. I tried and tried.

This was my emotional state when the processing parties began. I wonder sometimes if I would still be in that awful marriage if those parties never happened. It gives me the shivers to think so, but it may well be true. The love and support of those five women empowered me to finally leave that abusive relationship.

The day I left was the hardest day of my life. I rented a moving van, and drove the two hours back to our house, where I loaded everything of mine into the van, and left for good.

Then I drove to the resort hotel where Gina worked at the time. She had told me on the phone the previous night to stop by. "We'll go into one of the rooms," she said. "We'll be alone and you can cry." And that's what we did. I cried for a couple of hours, while Gina sat by me and listened. She didn't offer advice. She didn't congratulate me. She was just *there*.

On the day I went before the judge to get the divorce, Barbara went with me. We did a process beforehand, to center me and help me get clear on what I wanted to happen. We had to do it in the courthouse bathroom because there wasn't any other place to process; we couldn't find a hallway with any privacy. After the divorce was granted, we went to lunch and drank champagne. I toasted my new life through my tears, with Barbara holding my hand.

The girls' weekends, cruises, and playing in the singles scene with Lauri and Lee, completed the rest of my healing around my issues with men and control. Through processing, angel cards, singing Carpenters' songs, and drinking martinis, those weekends full of love allowed me to become whole again.

But just because I became healthy didn't mean I immediately became wise. I almost missed the love of my life when he showed up because he didn't seem like "my type."

Jack was a business colleague, one of the movers-and-shakers in Carlson Learning Company, where we were all distributors. He spoke at many of the conferences we went to, and since I was often one of the speakers too, we met on stage for panel discussions.

Soon we were talking to each other about putting together a new project to create e-learning courses—he in New Jersey and me in Chicago. We got to be great friends on the phone; for over a year we talked two or three times a week, long phone calls that would run for hours sometimes. Soon we were talking two to three times a day. Jack was sensitive, considerate, intelligent, and the kindest man I'd ever met. He was a man of real substance and integrity. He and his business partner were two of the most successful consultants in our industry, and I respected him tremendously. But more importantly, his heart was open. He expressed his feelings so freely. He was a widower with a teenage daughter. He had grieved for his wife and knew how fleeting life can be and how important it is to make your life count. We had many deep, soulful, spirit-filled conversations. Jack knew that the only thing that really mattered was loving someone. Although he didn't use those words in the beginning, all his actions indicated that what he wanted to do was love me.

As wonderful as this sounds, quite frankly it scared the hell out of me. Jack wasn't like anyone else I'd ever known. I kept pushing him away thinking this was "just a business relationship," when secretly I was afraid I was falling in love with him. How could I not?

I made up excuses why I couldn't entertain the thought of us being together.

"Oh, he's too old for me," I told the girls at one of our weekends, when they started to ask about our relationship, since he seemed to pop up in my conversation quite often.

"Really? How old is he?" asked Lee, looking puzzled. I told her. "Susan," she said gently, "that's only six years older than you."

"He's my business partner," I objected.

"So?" said Lauri. "What's wrong with that?"

"He's not the kind of guy I see myself with," I said, trying to make them understand, although I wasn't at all sure I understood what I was saying myself.

"And what kind is that?" asked Barbara. "The sweet, nice, loving, generous kind?"

"But he's so different from anyone else I've been with …" I said feebly.

"Exactly," said Gina.

"You're different now too, Sooz," said Nicki.

At the next girls' weekend Barbara invited a psychic to come and do readings for us, just for fun. When it was my turn, the psychic said, "There's a man in your life that you've already met, who is your forever love. He has all the qualities you want. Do you know who that could be?"

"Uh … Maybe, but I'm not sure," I said.

All the girls, who were listening, screamed at once, "Jack!"

Eventually I realized they were right and I was wrong. My

"type" used to be the big tough guy who would show me his tender side, although the ones I'd met never did. What if I "retyped" myself? What if my new type was a guy who was proud of his tenderness, sensitivity and inner strength? What if I told myself some new stories about men and relationships? What if I opened my heart to the finest man I had ever known?

I remember the exact moment when my blinders fell off and I realized that I was madly in love with Jack, and had been for a long time. I just couldn't hold it in any longer. By this time he had also become my best friend. When he asked me to marry him I knew it was the best thing that would ever happen to me. I immediately got ready to move to New Jersey.

The girls gave me a hilarious bridal shower, just the six of us, during one of our girls' weekends. Those gifts! I can't talk about the lingerie they gave me, I'm way too modest. It's a spit-pact. Let's just say some of those outfits—especially the one with the little black gloves—gave new meaning to the phrase "business casual."

The girls also had a lot of fun planning how they would "add" to the wedding, which was going to be a classy and sophisticated affair. This was shortly after our infamous Bad Girls routine at the talent contest, which we should have won but didn't. "We can do our Bad Girls routine at your wedding!" someone suggested; I believe it was Lauri. "You can't do that at my *wedding*!" I screamed, but I have to admit I was laughing. I knew they weren't serious.

The thing was, they *were* serious, unbeknownst to me. Because Jack had played the "john" for the Bad Girls routine at the talent show, the girls called him and asked if he wanted them to do a special reprise at the wedding. Jack is a conservative guy, and even more modest than I am. At first he said *No Way*. They wheedled. At last they got him to say *Maybe*. Then later he went back to *No*.

He was still saying *No-Maybe-No-Maybe* at the dinner reception after the wedding. The girls were having second thoughts by then too, because of the elegance of the affair. "My angels aren't sure," Barbara said. Jack's angels weren't sure either.

But after dinner, when people were up and dancing and a wild conga line snaked through the hall, Jack's angels changed their minds. He went up to the girls and said, "Okay, the sorority sisters' serenade is on."

They had brought their t-shirts, just in case, so they hurriedly put them on, and whisked the DJ out into the hall to give him the tape and tell him what to do. When he put the Donna Sommer music on, they swiveled their way onto the stage and did their whole routine.

My heart is opened!

It was a huge hit. The whole place was roaring with laughter. My make-up must have been a mess because I was crying and laughing so hard. Jack's business partner nearly fell off his chair. I lost count of how many people who had just met the girls and told me, "Your friends are so much fun!" Gina, as always the lead "singer," said she was given $7 in tips!

Jack's daughter Kristin, who was 20 then (she had been 18 when Jack and I met) came up to me afterwards when people were starting to leave. She was with a bunch of her girlfriends who had come to wish Jack and I well. "We've all decided," said Kristin, "We want to be just as connected as you and your friends are when we get older."

My heart smiled for her.

Angels.com: *Lauri*

Although I was in my forties when I met the girls, they've been with me through the most important relationship transitions of my life. When we first met, they stood by me as I was getting my divorce. Later they supported me through a passionate love affair that flamed fast and died faster, and then later still an engagement—that big honking diamond, as Nicki put it—that they knew was bad for me even when I didn't.

That engagement was to the last of my emotionally unsupportive men; it was the transition between my old style and the new one that was going to emerge.

I'd been trained well, you see. I truly didn't know that men could be emotionally supportive; I believed that only women were capable of this—and then only for men and children, not for each other. It was a revelation to me when I discovered how wrong I was.

When I was going through my divorce, my husband and I saw a marriage counselor in an attempt to save our marriage. This was shortly after my father died. During one of our sessions, my husband and I were sitting next to each other on the couch. The therapist asked me about my dad's death, and I spoke about him with tears running down my face. When I paused, the therapist looked at my husband and said, "Do you feel what your wife is going through? You're not reaching out to her to touch her or comfort her. You're just sitting there."

I think my mouth dropped open. That was the first time it occurred to me that I deserved support too, not because I was a failure or weak, but because I was a human being. It wasn't my husband's fault either; he had been well trained, too. His emotions were safely buried under tons of masculine stoicism.

My husband didn't understand why I needed my girlfriends. The only one of the girls he met was Barbara, and it stunned me when he told me that he didn't like her. I just didn't get how that could be possible. How could anyone not like Barbara? I think that was the last piece that finished our marriage.

It's not always easy to unlearn the habits of a lifetime. It takes time. It must have been hard for the girls not to shake me when I got engaged to a man who put me down continually, and to watch me overlook or excuse it every time he did. My kids didn't like him either. I kept saying, "You don't see what I see in him." That turned out to be the truth; what I saw wasn't really there, so of course they didn't see it. But although the girls never accused me, never made me feel stupid or guilty, they had a way of gently probing for the truth, bringing me closer and closer to being able to recognize it myself. Eventually I did, and they cheered.

It's not always easy to unlearn the habits of a lifetime. It takes time.

Then I became a swinging single! Well, not exactly, but I did have a lot of fun for the next couple of years, finding out who I was as a single woman. Susan was also single at this time (although she had met the man she was to marry, she just hadn't tumbled to it yet). We teamed up and went on some trips to Las Vegas together, and we joined the Single Gourmet, which is a dining club for singles. Every couple of weeks we'd go with a group to a different Chicago restaurant and each woman would be seated with a different guy each time. And I went on my first cruise; I went with Lee, and learned to love her even more than I already did. Lee can make me laugh with just one of her looks. My stomach hurt most of the time from laughing so hard.

But at heart I am a serious person, and I knew that what I wanted was a real relationship, one that would fulfill me forever. Although I had fun on the cruises and in Vegas, I had my doubts about the likelihood of finding the "right one" that way.

It's funny the way things happen. On one of our girls' weekends—this one at Buena Vista, Barbara's house in Florida—I talked about my desire for a serious relationship during our check in (or as Nicki calls it, the How You Doin). "I want to find my soul mate," I said. "I want the man who is right for me; I just don't know how to find him. But I have a feeling he is really close. He's out there right now waiting to meet me."

As I often did, I chose an Angel Card afterwards. I picked the Soul Mate card. The card said something like, "you are blessed because drawing this card means your soul mate is with you now or soon will be. You are joined as one."

Even though this kind of thing often happens with Angel Cards, it still amazes me. It amazed all of us because the language of the card was almost word-for-word what I'd said out loud.

Later that night when no one was looking I took the Soul Mate card out of the deck and put it in my purse. When I got home I put it on my bulletin board in my office, where I'd see it every day. (I didn't give it back until years later.)

It was very soon after that girls' weekend that my daughter brought the man she was going to marry to meet me. She was madly in love. She told me she had met him through an online dating service, and said, "You should try this, Mom."

"Hmm," I said. The next day I was talking on the phone to Lee, who was telling me her latest dating story of a man she had met on the same online site as my daughter. "You should try this, Lauri," said Lee.

I used to be a slow learner, but not anymore. Soul Mate card, guy waiting for me, you should do this—okay, I get it.

I put up a profile on the site. I described myself honestly, trying to convey my personality, but in reading others' profiles, I think people spend too much time describing themselves and not enough time describing who they want. That's what the Law of Attraction is all about: you attract what you put out there. Or to put it biblically, you reap what you sow.

I put a lot of thought into the description of the man I wanted to meet. This is what I wrote:

> *I am looking for a man who wants the most from life and from what love has to offer.*
>
> *Grand passion certainly has its place, but I believe lasting love requires a great deal more. I desire a relationship that is based on intimacy, caring, commitment, respect, affection, appreciation, mental stimulation, and an outwardly loving attitude of goodwill towards a partner.*
>
> *I am attracted to a man who knows what he wants out of life and has the passion, energy, attitude and drive to go after it. I like a man who stretches me emotionally, spiritually, mentally, physically, and passionately. Physical attraction/chemistry and verbal articulateness are very important to me. An entrepreneurial mind fascinates and stimulates me. I like a man who "knows himself" and appreciates and values what he has learned from life experiences. Personal growth inspires me.*

I met Randy just a few months later. We were married after a three-year courtship. He is handsome, financially comfortable, has a sense of humor, and most important of all, he is emotionally supportive of me. We have a beautiful and comfortable home. We have an adventurous life. My children love him. He loves my friends. In short, he exactly matches who I described online.

At our wedding reception the other five girls did our Bad Girls routine, just like they had at Susan's wedding, only this time they switched from the original t-shirts and wore a new t-shirt with garter belts instead. They also changed the song from *Bad Girls* to *We*

Are Family. More upscale! It was even choreographed, and again it was the highlight of the event. People talked about it for years. I thought Randy was going to choke he was laughing so hard.

I finally gave the Soul Mate card back. But I still have him.

On the Loose: *Lee*

My issues with relationships revolve around trust. I want to be in control of my own life, and when I get into a relationship I feel swamped by fear that I will lose that control to someone else, and he will let me down. The reason I'm afraid of this is because in so many of my relationships I *have* lost control, and the men I've ceded it to *have* let me down.

It's taken a long time for me to learn that this is a story I have told myself, and all I have to do to change it is to tell myself a different story. In fact, I am still learning to strengthen my story-telling skills. It's been a long and rocky path. Thank God the Bad Girls have been walking it with me.

When the Bad Girls first jelled I was in the process of divorcing my second husband. I was in despair because I truly cared about my husband, and I missed the man he used to be. He changed radically after his retirement; he became depressed, got hooked on anti-depressants, let his drinking get out of control, and finally started acting violently toward me and everyone else.

I wanted so much to help him, and I tried everything I could for years. But nothing worked. Finally I knew I had to consider divorce, although I had trouble making up my mind to really go through with it. What would happen to him if I left? How could I kick him when he was so far down?

It was the Bad Girls, especially Barbara, who helped me see that I was actually in danger—real, physical danger—by staying with him. We did a lot of processing around trust, but ironically the issue was never one of trusting men; it was about trusting myself to make the right decisions. Barbara's outside perspective reassured me as well. "You've got to stop waffling and leave, Lee," she said. "You need to get out *now*." She clearly saw the danger I was in when I could not. You never think something violent can happen to you, but of course, it can.

I knew that Barbara and the rest of the girls would be there for me. I knew I always had a safe place to stay. I could count on them, talk to them at any time, and tell them anything without fear of judgment. Without the safety net they held out for me, who knows…maybe I wouldn't have left in time.

So you'd think I would listen to the girls the next time I got into a relationship, wouldn't you? Well, I didn't.

I had developed a pattern. I got married, the marriage was good for a time, then went south. I tried to save what wasn't savable until I had to divorce. Then I enjoyed being single for a few years until I got lonely. I'd meet a man who paid attention to me and made me feel important, and I would cave and marry him. There would be some good times, but eventually he would let me down and I'd go through the process again. The only difference was that the good times got progressively shorter, and the hard times longer.

When I married for the third time, I had plenty of warning that I was doing it again. My heart told me, "I shouldn't be doing this," and the Bad Girls all agreed that my heart was right on.

Barbara asked me more than once, "Lee, what are you doing?" I ignored all of them and did it anyway.

Once I was married, they supported me all the way. When the marriage fell apart less than a year later, not one of them said, "I told you so." Not one of them even thought it. Instead, they just helped me sort through the gigantic mess he created. This one really took me to the cleaners—emotionally and financially. It cost me big time to get out of it. You know, when you don't listen when your angels whisper in your ear, eventually they have to shout at you to get your attention.

Now I am single again. But this time I'm loving being single. Being single doesn't mean being alone. I am dating and having fun. Who knew that you could have fun dating while in your sixties? The girls say with glee, "Lee's on the loose," because they love to hear my dating stories.

Nevertheless, they keep trying to fix me up; they're always on the lookout for me, wherever they go. I don't think they can help themselves. I don't mind; they might do a great job picking out the right guy for me. If the right guy really exists. Sometimes I think he does, and other times I'm not so sure. But I'm not stressed about it.

You know, when you don't listen when your angels whisper in your ear, eventually they have to shout at you to get your attention.

I discovered the online dating sites. I'm a match.com junkie. I advised Lauri to go online, and look what happened for her—she actually did meet Mr. Right. I think online dating is great. You don't have to meet anyone if you don't want to; you're in control. You can weed out the ones who would just waste your time, and yes, there are a lot of them. But so what? Looking is fun.

I'm a winker. If I see someone who looks good and whose profile is interesting, I just "wink" at them to let them know they caught my eye. I like to get winks, too. I'll get up in the morning sometimes and look at myself in the mirror and I look god-awful. But then I'll go to my email and I'll have three winks. I'll think, "Golly, that's pretty good. I must look better than I think!" Darn good for your self-esteem.

I've met some nice people, too, even if no one has been Mr. Right. Not yet, anyway. I know it's a long shot. And I'm cautious; I don't meet anyone right away, not until we've gotten to know each other through emails, then through a phone call or two. And of course I don't give out personal identifying details and if we do meet, we arrange to meet in a public place.

The biggest hazard of online matchmaking is that people sometimes lie. Maybe they start out thinking they're just highlighting their best qualities and down-playing their worst. Maybe they think you won't notice the discrepancies—or maybe they really believe their own lies; I don't know. They are hard to weed out, because you won't know they've been lying until you meet them.

My worst example of this happened to me when I'd only been doing match.com for a couple of months. I'd met this guy and we'd emailed and talked on the phone, and we seemed to really hit it off. He was witty, charming, sensitive, and a high-energy guy with lots of interests in common with me. The only drawback was that he lived in a different state, but he said he was willing to move for the right woman. So eventually we agreed that he'd come to visit me over a weekend. I made hotel reservations for him and told him I'd meet his plane.

I told the Bad Girls about this guy when we got together for one of our girls' weekends. I showed them his profile and his picture. Then I told them he'd be coming to visit me for a weekend. "What are you doing, Lee?" asked Barbara. "He sounds nice and he looks good, but *what are you doing*?" This is her favorite question and it's a good one. I am working on getting better at answering it.

"It's no big deal," I said breezily. "He can go back again. It's not a problem. I'm not going to be sleeping with him or anything. But I have to meet him somehow."

"Hmm," they all said.

The next Friday I was at the airport to meet him. I had his picture so I knew what he looked like…or did I? On match.com he said he was 6'1". I'm almost six feet so height is important to me. But then I spotted a guy whose face looked like him, only he was 5'8" at the most even though he was wearing cowboy boots and a cowboy hat—*not* a fashion statement that appealed to me. And he was at least ten years older than he had claimed.

"Dear God, don't do this to me," I thought. "Please let this not be him."

But of course it was. And his lies about his height and age were just the beginning. He was obnoxious on top of it. He laughed too loud and in the wrong places. He bragged about his money. He told me what he thought about everything, even when I didn't ask. He thought he was Mr. Stud Muffin. He couldn't keep his hands to himself. He didn't want to stay at the hotel, he wanted to stay at my house. He sulked when I said no.

By Saturday afternoon, I'd had enough. "That's it," I said, after another of his self-righteous remarks. "You have to go home. I'm taking you to the airport."

That was the only time I ever had anyone visit me from a distance. I'll never do it again. The Bad Girls were so right.

But he was an extreme example. Most of the men I've met are nice; just not always interesting. I sometimes think men have women write their profiles for them—maybe their sister or daughter—to make it look attractive to another woman. Their profiles can make them sound so exciting, but when you talk to them they put you to sleep.

Ah, but sometimes ... just recently I met somebody that I liked. His profile was good, his picture was good. We met for coffee, and that was good. Then we had a real date, and that went better than good. Our second date was nothing less than great. I thought, "Wow, this is getting exciting!"

Then two days after our great second date, I got an email from him that basically said, "Thanks, but no thanks." He said he didn't think our relationship could go anywhere.

I thought, "What the heck?" I was hurt, angry, and confused. I called Barbara, and she said, "Let's see what your angels say about this."

So I got my pack of Angel Cards out and spread them all over the bed. "What do I need to know about this situation?" I asked.

The card I picked out said something like, "Get ready for someone wonderful and powerful to come into your life. You will be happier than you have ever been before."

The hurt, anger, and confusion immediately went away. I took that card and stuck it in my bedroom mirror, where I would see it every morning. Then I went into my office, got on the computer and signed on to match.com. I winked at about twenty guys.

I was totally over it. I just put that other guy away and thought, "If there's somebody else out there for me, damn it, I'm going to find him. This wasn't the one, so what the heck am I worrying about him for? Get back out there again." And this time I listened to myself.

Now if I get discouraged again, I call Lauri. I listen to her talk about her life with Randy, who she met through match.com. I know there is someone out there for me. I know it. I may be on the loose now, but I won't be forever.

"We Are Family!"

Good Fun at the Jersey Shore

FIVE

If You're Not Having Fun Your Business Will Suffer

$\mathcal{F}$our of us—Gina, Susan, Lauri and Nicki—flew into the Southwest Florida Airport, to join Barbara and Lee for one of our much anticipated girls' weekends. Barbara and Lee were already in Florida and were picking us up at the airport.

Lauri worried there wouldn't be enough room for all her luggage, especially her shoes. (We'll talk about Lauri and her luggage later.) She kept calling Barbara on her cell phone and asking, "What car are you bringing? Are you sure it'll be big enough?"

"Just don't worry; we'll be there and it'll be fine," Barbara said each time.

It was more than fine. Barbara and Rick had a big long, white motor home which they drove from Chicago to Florida each year, and this was the monster that Barbara and Lee drove to the airport. It was a dazzling vehicle; it looked like a movie star's trailer.

The four of us were standing outside at the arrivals area, craning our necks to see if we could spot Lee and Barbara among the cars coming and going, when we heard a loud honk. It seemed to shut out every other noise. We looked up (so did everyone else at the airport) and there were Barbara and Lee hanging out of this enormous white thing, yelling at the top of their lungs, "Girls! Girls, it's us!"

People's heads swiveled to us, and you could tell by their faces that they were wondering who we could be. Were we rock stars? Billionaires? Should they get our autographs? We heard some of them whispering, "Who are *they*?"

And then they started to smile, as Barbara and Lee leaped out of the gleaming wheeled mansion and we all started hugging and squealing. That's something that frequently happens around us—people smiling when they see the six of us together.

The vibe we give off is not, "Hey, look at us, we're important." Instead it's, "Hey, we're having a good time! And so can you!"

Sometimes our girls' weekends are intimate gatherings, when just the six of us hunker down in a comfy place, wear our sweats and pour our hearts out to each other. In the beginning, when most of us were just starting our businesses, we couldn't afford to go on expensive jaunts, so we gathered at each others' homes.

Later, when each of us became more successful (although all of us have had our financial ups and downs), we sought out inexpensive ways to expand into the world. Besides tacking on girls' weekends to business trips, we found that cruises and Club Med vacations were usually within our means, especially if we only went once or twice a year. And when we did go out into the world, it didn't matter if we went upscale or downscale; the important thing was to have fun.

There's something contagious about people having fun. Although we don't look for other people to join us, somehow they always do. They find us. We'll be minding our own business and doing our own thing, and soon other people will be drawn into our circle; it's like we create this energy field.

Sometimes we consciously try to spread positive energy, but usually it just spontaneously seeps from our pores when we're together having fun. Positive energy is very hard to resist. Even curmudgeons can be overcome when there's enough of it around.

<hr />

Positive energy is very hard to resist. Even curmudgeons can be overcome when there's enough of it around . . . Men seem to be magnetized by happy women.

And no, we're not fun just because we drink martinis! We don't drink martini after martini until we're drunk. Usually just one—the perfect one—is enough. Cocktail hour with Bad Girl martinis is performance art, a part of our ritual of fun. We drink our martinis slowly, as if we are in a 1930s movie. You know, like those glamorous women who blow cigarette smoke sensuously over a martini glass and look so very, very chic. Too bad none of us smokes. Of course, today smoking wouldn't look chic; it would just look stupid.

If we're on a cruise or visiting a new restaurant or bar, we educate the bartender on how to make the perfect martini, just like the ones we make when we're on our own. Martinis in the 1930s were always made with gin, but we like vodka martinis, so that's another way we're not like Jean Harlow and Marlene Dietrich. Our martinis must be made with Ketel One Citroen Vodka—

so soft and lemony. Also, they must be very chilled, straight up, and the green olives must be stuffed with blue cheese. Yes, we are picky. But oh, they are so good! Just ask anyone who has watched us order them; many times other people at the bar will want what we're having. The bartender will get really good at making them by the end of the evening.

Not all of us were martini drinkers at first. A few of us had to be educated as well as the bartenders. Initially Susan was afraid to order one, because she was sure she'd get it wrong. "I'll have what they're having," she'd say. It took her several practices to get it right. The olives always tripped her up.

And Nicki, well, Nicki was a Miller Lite kind of gal. She'd never had a martini in her life before becoming a Bad Girl at the first business conference she attended. And that wasn't until the last day of the conference. On the first day, we went to the bar for cocktail hour and five of us had martinis, and Nicki had a Miller Lite. Then we went to dinner, where five of us had a glass of Chardonnay, and Nicki had another Miller Lite. "You have to learn how to drink with the big girls, Nicki," we told her. We badgered her and badgered her and finally she agreed to have a martini on the last evening of the conference.

We told everyone at the conference that Nicki was going to have her very first martini that night. Pretty much everyone showed up to watch Nicki be inducted into the Martini Club (we hadn't become the official Bad Girls yet). What a celebration it turned out to be. They almost ran out of vodka, and they did run out of blue cheese olives

Susan and Nicki still only drink martinis when the Bad Girls get together, and they certainly never drink more than one. Then

Susan returns to white wine, and Nicki, who feels she has educated her palate, drinks red wine. But neither of them would ever miss that first celebratory martini.

We have another drinking ritual that involves hot tubs. It began at a girls' weekend at Barbara's house in Florida. One night we drank White Russians while soaking in the hot tub, laughing and telling stories. The next time we had access to a hot tub during a girls' weekend we were at a resort hotel, and decided to take our Russians on the road, too—except this time we drank Black Russians. Black or White Russians, it doesn't matter as long as they are made with Ketel One vodka and Kahlua. Don't ask us why White Russians taste so good when you're soaking in a hot tub, but they certainly do. Just ask any of the many people we've turned on to this treat.

The only problem is that the Russians don't always stay in their glasses. In fact, they never do. *You* try to giggle, snort, and hoot without spilling; it's just not possible. They slosh over the top and end up in the hot tub with us, and in the mornings the hot tub looks like it's full of coffee lattes. One morning of a girls' weekend at a Club Med, we were lounging around the pool having our morning coffee (straight) after a night of Russians in the hot tub. The pool guy came by to clean the pool. "Oh my Lord," he said after one look. "What were you girls doing last night?" We said, "Oh, nothing."

But you know, all he did was laugh. "I wish I'd been there," he said.

It's not just pool guys that are drawn by our energy, it's all men. Men seem to be magnetized by happy women. We aren't that young anymore, and although we're all attractive, we don't pretend to be drop-dead gorgeous. And none of us, except Lee, are in the market for a new man. Lee isn't really looking either; most of the time she's having too much fun to look. Besides, she doesn't have to; they're looking at her.

They're looking at all of us. Although the one they look at the most is Nicki, probably because she is the youngest. At Susan's and Lauri's weddings, all the men wanted to dance with her. She had to beg to sit down. At many of the conferences, Nicki went around singing *It's Raining Men* because around her it was!

What men really like is women who are having fun. At one Carlson conference, Susan had three guys after her, only one of whom was Jack. This was before she knew Jack was interested, and when she still pretended they were just business friends. She might not have seen Jack's interest, but the rest of us did. It was obvious he was peeved about the other guys trailing after Susan. At one point, Susan, Jack, and another guy were standing together talking. Susan looked very serious. Jack looked determined. The other guy looked like a lovesick sheep. Nicki walked by humming *It's Raining Men*, Susan began to laugh, and the sheep guy joined in enthusiastically, although we're pretty sure he didn't know what he was laughing at. Jack wasn't laughing.

It's not just men; we draw in women, teenagers, and kids, too. We know that life is fun, and who doesn't want to be around that?

There's a piano bar in Chicago called *The RedHead* where we like to go when we're together. You walk right in and belly up to the piano, you're served a drink, and then you sing. Well, not everyone sings, but anyone can if they want to. We always want to. Strangely enough, when we sing everyone else joins in. And not because we've got great voices, that's for sure. It's because we sing with gusto.

You might think we'd get some disapproval as well as appreciation, because you know, sometimes we can be loud. But we've never had anyone give us dirty looks, or sneer at us, or sniff like the proverbial uptight librarian. All we get is people wanting to join us, to be a part of what we're doing. When we come into a place where we've partied before, we hear, "All right! Here come the girls!" And we sing back, "Here we are!"

We give people permission to have fun. A lot of people would like to go out and have outrageous fun and throw away their inhibitions, but what holds them back is their fear of disapproval. Some people seem to wear emotional straightjackets when they're out in public. We approve of fun, and this encourages them to take the straightjackets off.

Everyone wants to come to a great party, right? Especially if it looks like it's being held in a movie star's motor home.

Fun and Indecent Exposure: *Lee*

The Bad Girls have a good effect on others. It just seems to happen, whether we're playing or working. Maybe it's because we're all in the human potential field. After all, it's our job to affect people in positive ways.

I love my work because it is fun. At least, it's fun most of the time. And when it isn't, I find ways to change things so it is. This is a lot easier when I'm working with one of the other girls. We don't compete with each other; we collaborate, so we find ways to work together. This is us at our most effective—having fun and doing business at the same time. They are not mutually exclusive, as many people seem to think. If you're not having fun, your business will suffer. If you're not doing business, you're probably not having fun. And neither is anyone else.

Barbara and I were once hired to put on a seminar in Peoria, Illinois for 24 government attorneys. It started out as the most not-fun event ever. For one thing, not one of those 24 attorneys—all men—wanted to be there. They were there because they were required to attend. None of them were friends; in fact, from the way they interacted, I believe they all hated one another. The most charitable description of their relationship was they were fierce competitors.

And our seminar was about the benefits of cooperation!

Barbara and I mixed it up during the training. Sometimes I'd be in front and she'd sit in the back of the room, sometimes we'd switch, and sometimes both of us would be up in front interacting. We're both good seminar leaders, trained to elicit participation. We're good at the light touch and using humor to make serious points. We're used to lots of laughter and interruptions. We're used to liveliness.

Well, not this time. While Barbara and I talked, those 24 attorneys sat glued in their chairs with their arms folded across their chests, poker faces staring straight ahead. No matter what we did or said, we got no response. The only time the attorneys talked was at breaks, and they didn't actually talk, they just argued with each other. At the end of the break they'd take their seats and go back to looking through us.

It was a three-day seminar. At the end of the first day, Barbara and I made a bee-line to the bar. We needed a martini that day!

We looked at each other and said, "How are we going to make it through two more days?" Back in our dungeon-like hotel room, with its poor lighting and a small window overlooking a filthy alley, we reviewed possible tactics and agreed that it was unlikely any new tactics would work with this bunch of uptight men. Then we giggled all night because the whole thing was so ridiculous. What else could we do but laugh?

The next day was more of the same. Sullen faces, closed postures. The attorneys weren't actively hostile, at least not to us, but they were simply non-responsive, the very picture of passive-aggression. By 2 o'clock Barbara and I were exhausted, our normal energy sucked right out of us.

That's when I lost it. It was my turn to present up at the front. I could hear that I was starting to talk mechanically as I flipped transparencies on the overhead projector. (This was in the years past, before everyone had a laptop.) The topic I was covering was "how to have effective confrontations."

And a miracle—one of the attorneys made a remark!

"Why are you wasting our time with this?" he said, his voice dripping with patronizing contempt. "We love confrontation; it's what we are all about. That's what we get paid for."

I didn't stop to think about what I did next. I took the plastic transparencies in my hand and tried to rip them up. But I couldn't because they were plastic. Frustrated, I flung them on the floor instead. Then I turned my back to the class, smacked myself on the ass, and said, "You can kiss this!"

This was not professional behavior, of course. I shouldn't have done it. But when I turned around again, the stony poker faces were gone. Instead there were raised eyebrows and dropped jaws.

Barbara's mouth was especially wide. She caught my eye and mouthed her favorite question at me, "*What are you doing?*"

Then somebody laughed. And another person joined him. It spread pretty fast after that. I was laughing too, my frustration forgotten—or at least forgiven. And from that point on, the seminar went a hundred times better. I wouldn't claim that it was the best seminar we ever gave, but at least it had been rescued from disaster.

The other girls loved it when Barbara and I told them that story. We told it in a bar during a girls' weekend in Mexico some months later. We acted it out—Barbara's stone-faced attorney was especially funny—and as we got into the story, it wasn't just the other girls listening; we had drawn a little crowd. When I slapped my butt, the crowd shrieked with laughter. It wasn't that the story was that funny, it was that we had so much fun telling it. As the story proved, laughter is contagious.

I don't mind that I was the butt of that story—literally! Some of my favorite stories are when the joke is on me. You've got to take yourself lightly. We're all human, after all.

Even when I'm not with the girls, I store up my experiences so I can tell the girls later. We love to laugh about the absurdities of the human condition.

One of their favorites, and mine, is my water pill story. I had an appointment with a client in Sarasota, about 80 miles from my home in Fort Myers. Before I left the house I thought, "I should really go to the bathroom one last time, but no, I'll be fine." I was rushing, of course.

I got into my little Jaguar, drove a couple miles down I-75, and then stopped dead. There was an accident up ahead that had traffic grid-locked. I felt a twinge from my bladder, and started to pray that it was a small accident.

It wasn't. An hour and a half later, I'd gone maybe half a mile. I swear I could feel my bladder swelling, as if someone was blowing up a balloon inside me. Suddenly I remembered that I'd taken a water pill that morning. What was I thinking! The pants of my brand new powder blue silk pantsuit got tighter and tighter.

I looked at the people in the cars around me. They all looked relaxed and happy, chatting with each other, taking swigs from their water bottles or coffee cups. Just watching them drink made me feel worse. I was going to explode. Maybe I'd die of kidney poisoning right there on I-75.

Finally, I saw the next exit sign. Thank God! All exits off major highways have gas stations around them, or at least a McDonald's, right? Maybe I wasn't going to die after all.

It took another twenty minutes to reach the exit, each of them filled with agony. I sighed with relief as I drove off the freeway onto a small side road, which turned out to be one of the only side roads off I-75 that did not have a gas station or McDonald's along it. As I drove—no, flew—along the road, frantically looking for something that did not seem to exist, I suddenly knew I was not going to make it. If I didn't pee right then, I was going to damage something—probably something I needed to stay alive.

I pulled off on the side of the road. I looked for something to pee in, like a can or a Styrofoam cup, but I kept my little car clean. Besides, a Jaguar is not an easy car to maneuver in. I was going to have to get out of the car and pee outside.

There was a small stand of trees a short way away, but this is Florida. In Florida it is dangerous to go into the woods to pee;

there might be alligators or snakes or biting red ants. I would have to stay where I was.

Even though it was a small side road, there were cars passing by. Plus, I could still see the cars stuck on the jammed-up freeway, and I was sure the drivers could see me. I couldn't take down my pants; I might be arrested for indecent exposure. Yet how could I do this without looking ridiculous? My ego and its fear of looking bad was having a big argument with my screaming bladder.

I worked out a compromise between them. I positioned myself by the Jaguar, and leaned into the side window with my cell phone at my ear. I hoped anyone glancing my way would think I had merely pulled over to have an important conversation while standing outside the car.

Then I just let go and peed in my pants. I really had no choice. It seemed to take forever, and when I was done I looked like someone had thrown me in a lake. My powder blue pantsuit was now a much deeper blue.

I threw the pantsuit jacket on the driver's seat (I didn't care if it got wet—at least it would match the pants), got in the car and drove away—the other way, back toward home. I called my client and told him I was stuck in traffic and would have to reschedule. Then I looked at the gas gauge and saw that I was nearly out of gas!

Going the other way on the side road did lead to a gas station. It was probably the only one within miles, because there were at least twenty people there pumping gas. Self-serve only, of course. Meaning I would have to get out of the car.

This is when it struck me how funny this situation was. It hadn't been funny before, but now, without that awful internal pressure, I felt giggles start to pop out of my nose and mouth. "What the hell," I thought, and got out to pump the gas.

I stood there totally drenched and snorting with laughter, and looking around I saw that other people were also smiling. I'm sure they were wondering what had happened to me, or maybe they guessed I had wet my pants. But their smiles weren't mean. Nobody was snickering or pointing. They were laughing because I was.

We're all human, aren't we? We all go to the bathroom, and we all like to laugh. The fun is in how you tell the stories. I make a habit of having fun. No matter what!

Fun and Surprises: *Barbara*

Lee's not the only one who can tell funny stories, although she's probably the best storyteller of the Bad Girls. We all have funny adventures from time to time, and the best part about these stories is telling them to each other. Yes, we are serious about living a productive life that contributes to the common good. But as Lee says, fun and productivity are not mutually exclusive.

I'm probably the most physically adventurous of the girls. I was a tomboy as a child, and as a teenager and adult I've played on more sports teams than I can remember. So just because I'm in upper-middle-age now, I'm supposed to stop being who I am? I don't think so!

When Rick and I moved into our first home in Florida, it was lovely to be able to count on good weather, after living for so long in Chicago. Chicago's a great city, but the weather is not one of its main attractions. In Florida, everyone and everything is outside. From my front porch, I loved to watch the teenagers zoom by on their rollerblades. They looked so free and happy. After a while, I saw that not all of the rollerbladers were teenagers; some of them looked close to middle age. Maybe none of them were my age—I was in my mid-fifties at the time—but still, some were close.

"I want to do that," I told Rick one day, as we watched one young man do an intricate flip-twist-jump maneuver on the sidewalk.

"Are you nuts?" laughed Rick. "You'd kill yourself." He didn't take me seriously.

"No, really," I said. "I think I'll try rollerblading myself."

He looked up in alarm. "Honey, NO!" he said. "They're a lot more dangerous than they look. You could really hurt yourself."

Blah, blah, blah. As he argued on, I stopped listening. But he was obviously upset so I dropped the subject and didn't mention it to him again. He was traveling a lot at the time, and I didn't want him to worry about me while he was gone. And why would he worry? Because I was learning how to rollerblade.

While Rick was on his next business trip, I went out and bought some rollerblades. I also bought a helmet and kneepads, and got instruction from the people in the store. They didn't think I was too old; in fact, they seemed just about as excited as I was. "Just start out slow," the store manager said. "Practice inside your house, then in the garage, then on your driveway. And when you get out of the driveway, make sure you come by here and show us how you're doing!"

"What will Rick say when he finds out?" asked the girls. I kept them updated on my progress. They didn't think I was too old either; they were proud of me.

"I'll surprise him," I said. "I'll give him a surprise he can't refuse."

For the next couple of months I hid my rollerblades in my closet whenever Rick was home. When he was traveling, I'd strap on the rollerblades and skate my little heart out. I loved it, just like I knew I would. I skated by teenagers who would often give me the thumbs-up. When I went by the rollerblade store to show them how good I was, all the store employees came outside and applauded as I zoomed by.

When Rick called from the road, I teased him about the surprise I was preparing for him. "Come on, what is it?" he wheedled. "It wouldn't be a surprise if I told you," I said. "Will I like it?" he asked suspiciously. We'd been married long enough for him to know I sometimes took a few risks here and there.

"Oh, you'll love *this* surprise," I assured him.

Finally, when I felt confident of my rollerblading prowess, I decided to tell him. He had just come home from a trip, and we were outside on our private lanai having a glass of wine. "I'm ready to show you your surprise now," I said. "You sit here, and I'll be right back."

I went inside and put on all my gear—my rollerblades, my helmet, my elbow and knee pads. I took off everything else.

"Okay," I called. "I'm coming. But first you have to close your eyes."

He obeyed, and I skated out onto the lanai. As he heard me coming, his eyes flew open. Then his mouth followed. I skated around him in a spiraling circle, coming closer and closer. I even did a little hop and didn't fall down! *Hey*, I thought, *I'll have to try skating naked more often*. I felt freer than ever.

By the time I flopped down on his lap, Rick was nearly doubled over in laughter. "Okay, okay," he sputtered. "Go ahead and rollerblade, but promise me you won't go outside like that!"

He loves to tell this story. So do I. The first ones I told, of course, were the girls. Now they tell it, too. Funny stories take on a life of their own.

But it's not just telling our stories to each other, it's living them together, too. Every time the Bad Girls get together, we end up with more funny stories, often including how others react to us. You can have fun doing anything; even buying furniture can turn into a riotous adventure.

We have a thing about beds. On our girls' weekends, it's imperative that we have at least one king size bed available. Otherwise, how would we do our ritual "Coffee in the Big Bed" in the morning? Whoever is sleeping in the king bed knows that in the morning the other five girls will show up, coffee cups in hand, and flop down beside her, or lie across the bottom of the bed. The king bed is where we convene to plan the day ahead.

One time it was Lauri's turn to sleep in the king size bed. This was before she met her husband, and she was in the bed on the phone with her then-boyfriend—the one none of us liked—trying to have a romantic conversation. One by one, we came into the room and jumped on the bed with her, giggling as if we were still in high school. She kept saying, "Shhh!" but it was no use. We just got louder. Usually our silliness has a good effect on others, but I'm afraid it was the opposite with him. He thought we were a bad influence on Lauri. I guess from his point of view, we were!

So you see, we must have a king size bed. Queens are just not big enough. Because the beds in my cottage up in Michigan were old and small, when we set up a Bad Girls weekend there, we needed to buy a new bed. We decided to buy one on the drive up there.

There aren't a lot of places to shop near the cabin, so we had to call around to find a place that sold king size beds. The only one we could find was a bargain-basement place that was still a good thirty miles away. We called them ahead of time to make sure they had king size beds. They told us they only had one in stock, so we asked them to hold it and we'd be there soon to get it.

"Soon" was a little optimistic. None of us had been to the area before, and once we got there we determined never to come back. The GPS took us in circles through run-down neighborhoods where half the buildings had boarded-up windows or bars on the doors. We made sure the car doors were locked as we made one wrong turn after another.

When we finally found the discount furniture store, it looked as run-down as everything else in the vicinity. Inside, the saleswoman gave us a quick perfunctory smile. She seemed as dispirited as the store. Clearly, she didn't expect us to buy anything.

"We're here for the king bed," we said.

"Okay," she mumbled. She led us down a side aisle. "There," she said as she pointed to a big bed with green stripes. Obviously she was a woman of few words.

Well, of course we had to try out the bed, so we arranged ourselves as if we were having Coffee in The Big Bed—three of us side by side, the others sitting on the edge or lying across the bottom. We bounced up and down a few times. We switched places. And we started telling stories—laughing, giggling, even hooting at times. I can't remember now what was so funny, but then, I never can. We began to make our plans for the upcoming weekend. All that was missing was the coffee. Yes, this was the right bed.

The saleswoman watched us, her eyebrows raised in a bemused expression. "I guess I'll leave you girls alone for awhile," she said. As she walked back to the front of the store, Nicki whispered, "She thinks we're nuts, you know." I whispered back, "Well, we are, aren't we?" Snort, giggle.

The saleswoman kept a close eye on us from the front of the store. From her expression we knew she didn't have many customers like us. Yet some thirty minutes later when we finally got off the bed, the bored look had left her face.

"You girls have a good time?" she asked as we approached her. This time she had a real smile on her face, one that reached her eyes.

We assured her we did, and we loved the bed. As she wrote up our order, she said, "You know, when we were teenagers my big sister and I used to lie on her bed and talk like that. We sure had some good talks back then." Another smile came across her face, this one full of memory.

I would bet a lot of money that she called her sister as soon as we left.

Fun in a Hurricane: *Nicki*

Before I became a Bad Girl, I was nearly always working. Now, I loved my work and had fun doing it. But doing things just for fun…well, I didn't do that.

This changed with the Bad Girls. We went places and did

things just because they sounded like fun, and for no other reason. We even spent money on fun.

I never worried about money, and was okay spending it on the stuff I needed. I don't like the word "budget." It's almost as bad as the word "diet." Both sound like ways to control me. But spending money on pure fun was something new.

Spending my time on fun was even harder for me to grasp. It took me a long time to get used to it. Sometimes, Barbara would phone me and say, "Let's go get a massage (or a manicure, or go shopping, or whatever). Can you meet me in an hour?"

"Take the afternoon off to have a massage? Come on, I can't do that," I'd say.

"Why not?" she'd say. And most of the time I didn't have a good answer.

We all suffer from that darn Puritan ethic—even if our ancestors weren't Puritans. Mine were Irish and Italian Catholics, but I inherited the classic American "fun is sin" gene anyway. Although I was not as bad as Lauri, her Lutheran upbringing had made it even more difficult for her to change her ideas about fun. So naturally I turned to her to learn how to change mine.

The answer? Cruises! You know, you simply can't pretend to go on a cruise for any other reason than to have fun. This is difficult for a recovering Puritan. But if Lauri could do it, so could I.

It was Lee who exposed Lauri to the joys of cruises, back in the late 90s when they were both single. They came back with a lot of great stories, but probably the funniest was the one that happened before they even left. I wasn't there, but boy did I hear about it.

The night before the cruise, Lauri spent the night with Barbara so she'd be on time to catch the bus that was taking them to the port. Cruise ships do not wait for you. But she forgot to set her alarm, so she overslept. Then she misjudged how late it was getting, dawdling around with her then-boyfriend, who had come to pick her up to take her to the bus. Finally they flew out to the boyfriend's car and tore out of the driveway. Barbara said the squealing tires woke up her neighbors.

Meanwhile, the bus was waiting at the meeting place. It was past the time the bus was to leave, and everyone but Lauri was there. However, Lee had weaved her personal magic around the bus driver and got her to wait...and wait, and wait some more. But finally they couldn't wait any longer or they'd miss the boat, so Lee gave up. "Go ahead and go!" she exclaimed, throwing her hands up in the air and waving them about. Lee can get pretty dramatic.

The bus was just pulling out of the parking lot when Lauri, her boyfriend driving the car, sped into the lot. They saw the bus gathering speed, so the boyfriend pulled his car right in front of the bus and stopped. The bus couldn't go anywhere.

You'd think the bus driver would be furious, but Lee had told her so many Lauri stories by then that she was laughing instead. She laughed even harder as she watched Lauri try to pull her enormous suitcase out of the car's trunk and tow it toward the bus.

As the driver loaded the suitcase into the luggage compartment (with great difficulty), Lauri got on the bus and made her way toward Lee in the back. All the way down the aisle she apologized profusely, saying, "I'm so sorry for holding you up. Everybody, please forgive me. I'm so sorry." By the time she reached her seat next to Lee, the anxious frowns on the faces of the passengers had turned to grins. It's really hard not to like Lauri.

And as Lauri said later, "Besides, we made it to the ship right on time!" And Lee added, "Yes, with a whole 30 seconds to spare."

My first cruise did not start out quite as dramatically. It wasn't until we got on the ship that things started to happen.

It was late autumn of 2001, and the six of us had signed up for a four-day cruise of the Bahamas, leaving from Miami. Four of us from Chicago flew down to meet Barbara and Lee in Florida. In the Chicago airport Susan and I read a newspaper which mentioned a hurricane that might be developing in the Caribbean, but that didn't worry us; hurricanes were always developing, and most of them came to nothing. Right? Besides, I was newly single after the difficult ending of a ten-year relationship, and I was ready to party, hurricane or not.

The cabdriver who took us from the airport to the port also told us about the hurricane. "What?!" said Lauri in alarm, but the rest of us reassured her it would be okay.

It was a lot better than okay. The weather wasn't so great—rainy and windy—but there were so many things to do onboard ship that the weather didn't matter. We ate huge meals of delicious food, went to a movie in the middle of the day, had manicures and pedicures, gambled at the casino, sang karaoke at the bar, and of course at night we went dancing. I learned how to salsa dance with Lauri as my partner. Because I didn't know what I was doing, I kept looking at other people to see how they moved their feet and other extremities. Lauri would slap me on the arm and say, "Hey! You're dancing with me; stop looking at other people!" The next morning, I told the girls of our experience and how Lauri was my "jealous salsa partner," and that became another funny joke.

By the time we came into port at Nassau the hurricane was definitely coming. Now it had a name—Michelle. Our cruise was supposed to go on to Coco Cay, but that had to be cancelled. The cruise directors told the passengers we could disembark for an hour or so in Nassau, but I don't think they expected anyone to actually go. The rain was coming down sideways in sheets.

They didn't know Lauri. She had heard of the great deals on jewelry in Nassau, and she was on a mission to buy a gold Omega necklace. She had been talking about it for two days. Why would she let a little thing like a hurricane stop her?

"Come on girls, let's go shopping," she said, with that big happy smile of hers. "We'll probably get great deals because we'll be the only customers there."

Lauri is hard to resist when she's bent on one of her adventures, so we went. We ran through the town from shop to shop, shaking ourselves like dogs in the doorways, our hair plastered to our heads. People were boarding up their windows and doors, and the shopkeepers looked at us as if we were crazy. They were probably right.

Lauri found her gold Omega necklace in the last store we ducked into. They were on the verge of putting up the last boards and tried to tell us the store was closed, but Lauri didn't listen. To get rid of her, they sold her the necklace. They even smiled at her. I bought some jewelry, too; Lauri was right, there were some great deals.

Before we went back to the ship, I snapped a photo of Lee and Lauri hanging onto a palm tree so they didn't get blown away. The tree was bent over halfway. Lauri was wearing her gold omega necklace and clutching the store bag in triumph. Even though her hair was flattened against her teeth, you can see that smile.

As soon as we got back on board, they took us out to sea again, saying it was too dangerous to stay in port. They figured we'd be safer on the ocean if the storm reached us. Michelle had now reached Category 4 status and although no one was sure if it would reach the waters where we were, they were preparing to deal with that big of a storm.

It was bad enough as it was. The waves were around 50 feet. At one point they had to shut nearly everything down on the ship because we had to turn 180-degrees, which I guess is kind of a delicate maneuver. Even the elevator and the casino were shut down, which is never done. The atmosphere onboard got fairly anxious, and many people were getting seasick with the pitching of the ship.

Barbara had an anti-motion sickness wristwatch that we took turns wearing (yes, during a hurricane, motion sickness crept its way back). The watch sends electrical signals to your brain that tell you everything is just fine and dandy. Either this device really works, or we were too focused on having a good time in spite of the hurricane, because none of us got seasick, or even anxious. Pretty soon Barbara had lots of friends wanting to borrow her watch.

After they opened things back up, Lauri turned to me and said, "We better go shopping now at the duty-free shops, in case they close everything down again. I want to get some of those huge bottles of booze; they make great Christmas and hostess gifts."

Again her enthusiasm infected me, and we held onto the walls as we made our way to the duty free shops, where I bought at least six bottles of Bailey's Irish Cream, some specialty rum, some banana liqueur, and I think a couple bottles of Grand Marnier. It's hard to remember, but it's safe to say I bought a lot of booze. Every time I thought I was done, Lauri would pick up another bottle and say, "Oh, look at this great price! We've gotta get some of these, too!"

"But how will I get all this onto the plane?" I protested.

"I'll put some of yours in one of my suitcases," she said. "I can always find room."

But as it turned out, we missed our flight home to Chicago because we were stuck out at sea an extra day because of the hurricane. Then Lauri decided to stay in Florida a few extra days, so I had to carry all my booze home by myself.

Standing in line at the airport, I prayed that they'd just let me through, because I didn't want anyone to see how much booze I had in my bags. I felt like a closet alcoholic, or maybe I should say a suitcase alcoholic. At that time, there weren't restrictions on liquids in carry-on bags; what in the world would I have done!

They probably picked up on my anxiety, so that's why they chose to stop and search me. They held up the plane while they went through everything. Every single clanking bottle was on display. I told the security person, "You see, I have this friend, and she made me buy all this booze." He and the other passengers, who were getting antsy, just looked at me. Then I said, "I've been stuck on a boat for a couple of days; please don't take my dirty underwear out of my bag." That didn't work either.

Finally I thought, "What would Lee do in this situation? Or Barbara, Gina, Susan, or Lauri?" They would laugh, I decided. So that's what I did. And eventually I was allowed to get on the plane.

Why is Lauri such a hilarious traveling companion? It's because she takes herself lightly and seriously at the same time. What a gift. Always late, usually frantic and over packed, she goes at things head-on at top speed, with ferocious energy and focus. And yet, she's the first one to relax and laugh at the goofiness that ensues when she takes off on yet another adventure.

It doesn't matter how much hilarity or chaos she causes, she'll continue to be this way until the day she dies. I bet she'll make that cliché "late to your own funeral" come true. Everyone will be sitting there, all solemn and sad in the church, and we'll wait, and wait, and just as everyone is ready to get up and leave, the pallbearers will rush into the church and run down the aisle carrying the coffin aloft. Probably the coffin will burst open and all the shoes and clothes that have been jammed inside will come flying out. Wherever the rest of us are, in the church pews or up in heaven, it's a sure thing we'll be laughing.

Lauri is the most fun person I know. Even a hurricane can't faze her. God, I just love her.

Fun and Adventure: *Lauri*

When I was growing up, and when my kids were growing up, I thought life was a serious matter. I still think life is a serious matter, but now I believe that laughter, not fear, is a better way of dealing with it. It's only when you take yourself lightly that you can get anything meaningful done.

Yes, sometimes I'm funny. But I'm not the only one; all of us are funny, especially when we don't mean to be. When you love and totally accept people, their funny traits just become endearing. It's part of the magic.

**It's only when you take yourself lightly that
you can get anything meaningful done.**

That's why I don't care when the Bad Girls tease me about being late, or over-packing. For instance, when we spent a week in Arizona, I brought a whole suitcase full of nothing but shoes. I'll probably never hear the end of that one. In my defense, we were there a whole week! First we went to a professional conference in Phoenix that lasted four days, and then we tacked on three more days to stay at a ranch in Sedona, just the six of us. We planned to go hiking, ride horses, visit the hot springs, and go dancing at night. I needed hiking boots, riding boots, tennis shoes, Coffee in the Big Bed slippers, a couple pairs of dancing shoes, and of course business shoes to match the suits I brought for the conference. Yes, that takes up a lot of room, but I want my feet to look good!

The girls can laugh at me for my love of shoes, but they have their own stuff, too. Take Susan, for instance. Susan is deeply spiritual and interested in all sorts of metaphysical subjects. But sometimes she is so metaphysical she loses touch with reality. Jokes tend to escape her if they depend on popular culture, because Susan doesn't really do popular culture.

When we went horseback riding in Sedona, we arranged to go

on a two-hour trail ride through the mountains. We're all "horse people" and knew how to ride, but we didn't know the Sedona trails and needed a guide. Our guide was a grizzled cowboy who looked as though he slept on his horse every night. He didn't say much, mostly grunting, and when he did speak he sounded as if he'd been smoking four packs a day for fifty years. Nicki started referring to him as "Curly" after the Jack Palance character in the movie *City Slickers*, which had come out a few years earlier. The guide's name was really Tom, but pretty soon we were all calling him Curly—behind his back, of course.

Except that Susan, who had never heard of *City Slickers*, didn't get that "Curly" was a joke. While we were on the trail, I said to the girls, "Next time we stop, let's ask Curly to take a picture of us." (I'm the unofficial group photographer.) When we stopped, Susan went up to the guide and said, "Curly, could you take our picture?" The rest of us nearly fell off our horses laughing. As for Tom/Curly, he seemed taken aback at first, but when we explained the joke, he smiled for the first time that day.

"Ladies, don't worry about it," he said. "If you want me to be Curly, that's who I am."

Curly let me take his picture as many times as I liked that day. He was flattered that I considered him photogenic. The girls are always telling me that I get a little carried away when I have a task. "She's on a mission again," they'll say. Or sometimes they'll say, "Look out—another Lauri adventure!" Okay, but if I don't take the pictures, who will?

But they're right that I do get so focused on what I'm doing that I can get carried away sometimes. While we were horseback riding in Sedona, I became focused enough to nearly fall off a cliff. Curly led us up this narrow winding trail along the side of a cliff. I followed directly after him, and the rest of the girls were some ways behind us. It occurred to me this would make a great photo op, so I turned my horse toward the girls coming up the trail to take their picture. "Okay girls, look up and smile. Catch up, Susan. Come on, Nicki, bunch in." I was having trouble getting them all in the picture. To get them all in, I urged my horse backward a bit. And another bit. And another, until Barbara said, in her calmest voice, "Lauri, stop right now or you're going off the mountain."

It's a good thing she got through to me, because when I looked behind me I saw that my horse's rear hooves were close to the precipice of the cliff. I nearly shrieked, but just then "Curly" turned around to see what was going on. "Don't kill my horse," he barked.

This struck us all so funny that we laughed hysterically even while I was gingerly urging my horse away from the cliff edge. We continued to giggle and snort all the way down the mountain trail, every time someone would repeat, "Don't kill my horse!"

But I digress. I was explaining that the other girls are funny, not just me. Barbara is funny because she thinks she can do things that would scare the pants off anyone else. She takes real, physical risks as if they're nothing. It drives her husband crazy. But we've learned to accept it, because although she sometimes overestimates her abilities, she always seems to survive despite herself.

And Gina is funny because of the way she sounds when she makes one of her pronouncements. It may be her *Sopranos*-type accent, or the way she sticks out her well-endowed chest when she announces something, or because her pronouncements are never about anything truly important but it takes you a while to get that

"Don't kill my horse!"

because of the way she says them.

Before one of our Bad Girls weekends in Florida, Barbara decided to learn how to pilot the *Pink Day*, a 24-foot motorboat she and Rick owned and docked at the marina attached to their house. Usually they hired a captain to take them boating, but Barbara being Barbara, she wanted to learn how to do it herself. She hired the captain to teach her, and planned to surprise us by taking us—all by herself—across the inlet to Shuckers, her favorite little dive, for lunch.

"Great!" we said, as she told us the plan for the afternoon. We believed her when she confidently said, "I know how to do this now." We piled gleefully into the boat, eager for lunch and whatever adventure awaited us. It was a glorious day, and Barbara was at the helm! I, of course, was taking photos. Gina and Nicki made us laugh at their impersonation of an Italian waiter, Susan dreamily lifted her face to the sun, Lee kicked off her sandals and wiggled her toes to show off her toe polish, and Barbara frowned in intense concentration as she tried for half an hour to maneuver the boat away from the dock.

Finally, she got the boat into open water and pointed in the right direction. "I'm fine on the water," she assured us. "It's only the docking part that takes me a little longer." She told us to get ready for takeoff.

Gina and Nicki stopped horsing around and sat down. Gina sat alone on the seat in the front of the boat. "I love boating," she declared, although as far as I knew, she'd never gone boating before. Barbara hit the throttle and the boat leaped forward, throwing Gina backward onto the floor of the boat, her bare legs splayed out in a perfect "V" in the air. One leg starboard, one leg port. (See, I know boating lingo too.)

"Boating! We're boating!" she called, in her Gina-the-Announcer voice.

Of course, we all cracked up—except for Barbara, who was trying to be the serious captain. "What are you doing?" she yelled. "Close your legs!"

We were still laughing when we reached the dock, and continued laughing for the forty-five minutes it took Barbara to get the boat in position to tie up. Shuckers was right on the dock, with windows facing the water, so the patrons inside had a great view of the show. As we went in the restaurant, we called out, "Boating! We're boating!" Since they were already laughing, this just made the Shuckers customers laugh harder. It was easy to join them. Shuckers gave us each a complimentary margarita as thanks for the entertainment.

To this day, no matter what we're doing, we'll mimic Gina, saying, "Shopping! We're shopping!" or "Swimming! We're swimming!" Gina with her legs V'd in the air will float through our minds, and we will laugh some more.

On a boat or on a horse, we're all funny. And no matter what Nicki says, I won't be late to my own funeral. I wouldn't want to miss any of the fun.

Fun and Being Risqué: *Gina*

There's something about Bad Girls fun that is freer than other kinds. I can let it all hang out when we're together because I know the girls are not going to judge me. I don't worry if other people might judge me because the girls have my back. The thing is, no matter how silly we get, other people *don't* judge us. Instead, they seem to get sucked into our fun and end up being silly themselves.

Like at Susan's bachelorette party. It was held in New Hope, Pennsylvania, where Susan had moved with Jack. New Hope is an old historic town with an active arts community and many charming shops. It's just the kind of place that Lauri cannot resist, so of course we went shopping on the morning before the party. We wandered over the wooden bridge that connects New Jersey, where our hotel was, to Pennsylvania and into the heart of New Hope.

Lauri and Nicki were hoping to find good buys on artsy jewelry, Barbara was thinking about horse prints, or even originals, and Lee said she needed a new handbag. I thought I might find something for Guy, something personal, even intimate, but I didn't have anything specific in mind. But mostly we wanted to find something extra for Susan; something silly that would make her blush. Susan is so cute when she blushes.

Maybe we should stop putting our intentions out there until we think them through, because the Universe seems to take us seriously—that Law of Attraction again! The first place we wandered into was a shop that sold sex toys, although we didn't know that until we started to look around and saw peckers and boobs everywhere. Forget the jewelry, handbag, and horse prints; we had so much fun playing with the toys that we never got to any of the other shops. Our adventure in this shop was definitely blush-worthy. We left with a discreet plain pink bag filled with not-so-discreet party items.

That night at the party we didn't wait long to use them. While standing at the bar ordering our signature martinis, Barbara snuck four hopping peckers out of the pink bag, wound them up and let them loose on the bar. These little guys—an erect pecker with two balls at their base—are about 2 inches tall and made of neon pink plastic. When wound up, they move up and down in a suggestive rhythm. When Barbara set them off, they scooted down the bar, madly humping as they careened into glasses, bottles, and other peoples' fingers.

Hopping peckers are the best ice breakers I've ever seen. Within minutes, everyone standing at the bar—pretty much the whole party—became good friends.

Then one of us—it wasn't me, I think it might have been Nicki—broke out her orgasm button. These are like those big red buttons sold by Staples, about 2-inches around. In the middle of the button is a red light, and when you push it, it makes the sound of a woman having an orgasm. A *big* orgasm, with noise that fills the room for at least twenty seconds.

We had purchased six of these buttons, one for each of us, which we were carrying in our purses. We hadn't discussed what we would do with them; we just trusted that the right moment would come. Nicki decided it had, and she sneaked her button out of her purse, held it underneath the bar where no one could see it, and pushed the button.

Things got pretty wild after that. We all got out our buttons, and had dueling orgasm contests. Then we passed the buttons around so that everyone could try. Orgasms echoed throughout the rest of the night, often showing up at the most inopportune times—like at the end of someone's heartfelt speech about how much they loved Susan. Then, "ooh, pant pant, aahh, gasp, uhhh …"

I still have my orgasm button, hidden in my dresser drawer. I hide it because I don't want what happened to Lee and her orgasm button to happen to me.

Lee put her orgasm button on a shelf in her closet, and then forgot about it. One day her two little granddaughters, ages five and seven, came to visit, along with their mother, Lee's step-daughter. The girls liked to play dress-up with Lee's clothes and shoes, and went to play in Lee's closet.

Lee was in the kitchen when she heard, "Ooh! Ahh! Oooh!" coming from her bedroom, reminding her that the orgasm button was in the closet. Trying to be cool so the girls wouldn't think it was a big deal, she strolled into the bedroom.

"Nana, what is this? Who is making these noises?" said the seven-year-old.

"Oh, nothing," said Lee. "It's just a toy. Let's put it up."

"But what is it, Nana?" said the five-year-old.

"Really, it's just a toy."

"Can we play with it?"

Sometimes the devil enters into Lee. She has an impish sense of humor, and I think she enjoys her reputation as a spicy lady.

"I'll tell you what," she said to the girls. "Your mom is in the other room on the phone. Take the button and go up behind her—don't let her see you—and then press the button."

This, of course, appealed to the girls, so they sneaked up to their mother and, "Oooh, aaahh" blasted her right out of her chair. The girls fell down on the floor giggling.

"What the …?" shrieked their mom, when she could speak. "What is that? Where did you get it?"

"In Nana's closet."

"I told you not to go in there! You never know what you're going to find in Nana's closet!"

Lee always laughs when telling this story, and I'm sure she laughed when it happened, but she did admit she cleaned out her closet before she let her granddaughters play in there again.

Every one of us Bad Girls has a story about those orgasm buttons, but Lee's is the only G-rated one. So that's the only one I'm going to tell. I know I said that fun is freedom, but a girl still needs to keep some things a spit-pact secret.

Fun and Living in the Light: *Susan*

When the Bad Girls first met, we ranged in age from 50 to 25. It's now over twenty years later, and the math is clear. We're not young. So? Not only are we having *as much* fun as we did then, we're having *more* fun. Why do people think fun belongs to the young? It doesn't. It belongs to all of us, if we choose to accept it. The Bad Girls always accept.

Just a year or so ago, we arranged a girls' weekend at our beach house on the Jersey shore. It was Labor Day weekend, the last great hurrah before the autumn winds. People crowd the sidewalks and the beaches. The shops and restaurants are jammed. And all these people are intent on one thing: having fun. We fit right in.

I don't remember why, but we agreed to bring our Bad Girls shirts with us. Maybe we had a premonition we'd need them, but I think it's more likely that by bringing them we triggered the Law of Attraction.

On the morning of our last full day at the shore, we split up into three groups. Lauri and I went shopping (with Lauri shopping is always on the agenda), Barbara and Lee went to the beach, and Nicki and Gina decided to get their nails done. Everyone wore their shirts.

Because the nail salon was only a few blocks down the main street from our house, Nicki and Gina set off on foot. Now, the shirts alone would have gathered them a few stares, but in addition, Gina has a way of walking that is unique. She holds her head up, shoulders back, and sticks her butt out, making her boobs—which are huge anyway—lead the way. It's a proud woman strut that says, "Here I am, and I am gorgeous." And she is. You could tell others agreed with her because all the way to the nail salon cars honked and people leaned out of their windows and waved.

Gina and Nicki responded by strutting their stuff even more. Nicki tried her best to rival Gina even though she knew she was outgunned in the boob department. Two Italian women together can be outrageous if they're given any encouragement.

They were still feeling pretty proud of themselves after they had their nails done. I know this because Lauri and I ran into them on the street outside a little Italian deli and they told us all about it. While we were talking, Barbara and Lee showed up from the beach, and since we were all hungry we decided to go into the deli and get some food for a picnic.

The ability to have fun wherever you are isn't often seen as a spiritual quality, but that's because we don't look deep enough. Having fun is living in the Light. It's creating positive energy and spreading it around.

The name of the deli was Mario's, and Mario himself was behind the counter when we walked in, all six of us togged out in Bad Girls t-shirts and laughing hysterically at Gina and Nicki's story.

I think Mario fell in love with us right then. He grinned all over his sweet and swarthy face. He wiped his hands on his apron and said, "And what can I get for you 'bad girls' today?" His voice was pure New Jersey Italian.

Barbara started to order some salami, saying, "Mario, we'd like …" but Nicki stopped her.

"You can't say his name like that," she said. "It's not Mario, it's Maaariio," rolling her r's and giving it an authentic New York twist. I wish I could talk like Nicki and Gina, but I can't, and neither can Barbara, Lauri, or Lee.

"We want stuff for sangwiches," Nicki said to Mario, who grinned at her. "Sangwich" is Italian-English for sandwich.

Mario began gathering meats, cheeses, olives, peppers, and I don't know what all, most of it made by Mario himself. "You need some of this," he said, and gave us all a taste. We agreed that we did need some. "And this," he added. By this time his wife had joined him behind the counter, and she started piling stuff on, too. She was just as cute as he was, a short stout Italian lady in a black dress.

"And what are you Bad Girls doing here?" asked Mario, as we stuffed our purchases into bags—we had enough for three or four picnics. We explained about our Bad Girls weekends. Mario thought we were the funniest things he had run into in a long time.

Of course, Lauri had to take a photo, so Mario and his wife came out from behind the counter and posed with us while another customer took our picture with Lauri's camera. Mario was right in the middle, surrounded by those six Bad Girl t-shirts. "Me and my Bad Girls!" he laughed.

We got more encouragement after we left Mario's, when Barbara and I decided to stop by a nearby liquor store to get some Kahlua for our Russians. The liquor store was sort of attached to a little restaurant and bar. As we stood at the checkout counter, we could see a stage and a tiny dance floor in the bar. Although it was only noon, there were already some guys at the bar. We could see them laughing as they eyed us and our shirts.

"Hey, we have Karaoke tonight," said the guy manning the cash register. "You girls should come back and perform—and be sure to wear those shirts." The guys at the bar echoed the request. "Yeah, come on back," they called.

That was all we needed; we love to sing, we love to move, and especially we love to be silly, so karaoke is an art form made for us. Barbara said at once, "Sure, we'll be there!"

During our five o'clock cocktail hour we practiced our routine. Well, sort of practiced; there was a lot more giggling than actual practice going on. By eight o'clock there we were at the tiny restaurant/bar, togged out in our shirts and with our Donna Sommer CD in hand. Ready for fun!

What we didn't know was that the audience and the performers were local Karaoke regulars, and they were serious about their art. As we watched one after another get up and sing beautifully, flawlessly executing intricate movements with grace and ease, we started to get a little nervous. "Girls, I don't think we should do this," Gina whispered across the table. "Maybe we can sneak out," added Nicki, looking toward the door. She glanced down at her Bad Girls t-shirt with its Kahlua stain on the right boob.

But the hesitation was temporary. Somebody, probably Barbara, said, "No, it'll be fun," and that magic word galvanized us again. Gina's cold feet suddenly warmed up and she led us onto the stage, strutting her stuff just like she'd done earlier on the street.

We laughed and jiggled, mugged and giggled through the song, at times running into each other because we had forgotten the right steps. In short, we weren't so great. Here's the great thing, though—after a few minutes of stunned silence, that audience was right with us. They laughed and clapped, even cheered a little. Not for our less-than-adequate performance, but for the sheer enjoyment we showed. They clapped for the fun.

The ability to have fun wherever you are isn't often seen as a spiritual quality, but that's because we don't look deep enough. Having fun is living in the Light. It's creating positive energy and spreading it around. We're not really Bad Girls; we are Light Workers.

I still visit Mario's Deli whenever Jack and I are at the Jersey Shore. The photo that Lauri took that day hangs in a prominent place, right by the cash register. Lauri made it into a card and sent it to him, signed *For Mario, with love from the Bad Girls.*

The spirit of fun lasts a long time. Maybe forever.

Fun at Mario's Italian Deli

Together at Rainbows for All Children **Canvases and Corks** *Gala*

SIX

Our Mission: Have Fun, Make Money and Do Good

*I*s it just our egos that make us think we're special? Or are the Bad Girls really unique and different?

Well, we are and we aren't. None of us individually are more special than anyone else, but together we have created something that is. We didn't set out to do it; it began as luck (we call it Divine Intervention), continued through persistence and consistency, and is maintained by a focus on positive energy.

We are unique because each individual is unique, but that doesn't mean that others can't do what we have done. If this weren't true, we wouldn't be sharing our story.

Today we see a huge growth in social media like Facebook and Twitter. People are hungry for connection. But social media can only go so far. To create deep and lasting connections, you need more than a social platform. You need physical, emotional, psychological and spiritual components. And that is what we have.

Our initial connection was based on business interests, but it quickly expanded to include all areas of our lives. Even though we didn't meet until we were adults, are from different areas of the country, and vary widely in age, we formed the same "best friend" bonds that you would with a friend you had since you were a little girl.

To create deep and lasting connections, you need more than a social platform. You need physical, emotional, psychological and spiritual components. And that is what we have.

How can others replicate this bond that we share? We think there are four essential components, mirroring the chapters in this book.

The first is being willing to share who you really are, down to your toes—to be open, real and vulnerable in the absolute faith that you are loved and valued, no matter what. Along with this is the commitment to love and value each other, again no matter what. Yes, we may make mistakes, do foolish things, experience despair, but we are secure that our fellow Bad Girls see through these failings to the unmatchable beauty within.

One of the primary tools we used to achieve this closeness we called *The Enrichment Process™*, which we believe benefits many people. Processing helped us to redefine ourselves by internalizing new and better stories. But it's not the only tool available, and it's not a miracle path to perfect friendships, either. It's a means, not an end. Maybe a reader of this book will come up with another way that is just as good. That would be fun; we are suckers for learning new things, especially those that help us become more aware.

The second component that makes the Bad Girls who we are is closely related to sharing. We nurture and support each other through the transitions of our lives. We listen with our hearts as well as our minds. There is no room for pettiness, backstabbing, or jealousy. These problems have simply never come up for us. Although we work in the same competitive industry, we don't compete with each other. We know that collaboration works better for everyone. We practice what we know. We even hire each other for projects with our clients!

Third, we enjoy our lives; we have fun! We take ourselves seriously *and* lightly, at the same time. This sounds like a paradox, but it's not. Having fun means we are always looking for the positive, and when we find it, we spread that positive energy around. We laugh a lot. We don't have to spend lots of money or travel to exotic places; there is richness of experience everywhere, such as furniture stores and Italian delis.

The more you laugh, the more you find to laugh about. Life is so absurd and so beautiful! Joie de vivre is contagious. We are like twinkling little magnets, drawing people toward us because we are having so much fun. We bring the light within us out, and the nature of light is that it spills over everyone. Then guess what happens? All that joyful energy expands and rebounds on us, creating more. It just keeps on giving.

Finally, the Bad Girls connection has endured because we are committed in terms of the time and energy we devote to it. We have made it a priority; for over twenty years we have gathered two or three times a year, sometimes more. When we get together, wherever we are, we have developed consistent patterns and rituals that sustain us and anchor us to our joint identity. Rituals are a vital part of community building; they create a sense of belonging. It doesn't matter what the rituals are, as long as they mean something to you. Ours are doing the angel cards, drinking a special Bad Girls martini, doing a process, and of course singing and dancing. Together these rituals address our physical, emotional, psychological and spiritual foundations. When we do them we remember again who we are and how much we love each other.

Although we work in the same competitive industry, we don't compete with each other. We know that collaboration works better for everyone.

So here we are, the Bad Girls. We are six women who see ourselves as light workers—passionate about healing, restoring, and helping people discover their individual paths to wholeness. We come together a few times a year to work on our psychological and emotional issues, nurture and support each other, laugh and have fun, and practice the rituals that remind us why we're here. We do this in order to refresh and rejuvenate so we can go back into the world to give what we've learned, by doing the work we have been called to do. You can call it management training if you like, but it is really how to help people be more kind, compassionate and loving.

Here are more stories of us doing just that.

We Have Enough: *Nicki*

I used to stress out about not having enough time to volunteer for worthwhile causes, or enough money to make a dent in the world's problems. I'd watch TV shows like *Extreme Makeover: Home Edition* with jealousy, not of the people who got the home makeover, but of the people who got to help them. I fantasized about which charities I'd support if I won the lottery. I'd read any article featuring people like Brad Pitt and Angelina Jolie and how they used their money and celebrity to help others. When Oprah Winfrey created the Leadership Academy in South Africa I tried for weeks to think of a way that I could meaningfully contribute to her efforts.

I did do some things. I was delighted when Lauri proposed the Bad Girls as a group contribute to the Chicago-based international charity Rainbows For All Children that helps children impacted by the emotional loss of death, divorce, parental incarceration, parental deployment, or a natural disaster such as Katrina. Initially, she asked for each of us to make a monetary donation. Who knew she would go on to create a Women's Board, to which the six of us became founders!

I love animals, especially dogs—I have two 4-legged boys of my own—and I donate to the Humane Society. If I had more land, I might offer to foster stray dogs, because I would probably adopt them!

I am passionate about improving the environment, and have gone green in my own small way. I set up a composter in the backyard, plus put in a couple of rain barrels so I'm reusing rainwater in my garden and for my flowers.

161

So it's not like I did nothing; it's just that I wanted to do more. I wanted to make a big difference, not just a small insignificant gesture.

And then at one Bad Girls weekend we spent an afternoon helping each other with some business projects, and it hit me: I was already making a big difference.

I facilitate trainings, and the reason I love what I do is because it does exactly that—it makes a huge difference in people's lives. I am set on fire when I see an "aha" appear in someone's eyes, and I know that something I said or demonstrated gave them an idea on how to do what they do better than they've done it before. I feel proud and humble at the same time; I'm grateful my skills can be used in this way.

Each training session is a new adventure. It doesn't matter if I've done the same leadership training or taught a team building exercise I've done twenty times before because each time is different. You never know who will be there, and what empty spaces in their hearts may be filled.

So many times the people in my training classes don't want to be there in the beginning. They've been told to attend by their company, and like most of us, they resent not being given a choice. Nine times out of ten they come in with attitudes. They're thinking *I don't want to be here. I'm missing calls. I'm getting behind.*

It's such a thrill when you see their attitudes change, and they recognize that they have been given an opportunity to fix something in their life that may not be working well. Or they may learn something about themselves that had been hidden from them before.

I flip switches in people's heads, turning on a light they didn't even know was there. They come in stuck in darkness, thinking *I don't need this, it's stupid*, and when I'm able to facilitate their learning, they become unstuck.

And with the Bad Girls connection, my abilities are multiplied. It's not just me, all five of us have the same mission. Through our collaboration we have helped hundreds, maybe even thousands, of people live more meaningful, joyous, kind, and loving lives. And because their lives are enhanced, so are the lives of the people they touch, and the multiplication continues.

I love sharing our respective skills at the Bad Girls' weekends. I had my own "aha moment" when Susan taught us about webinars. She has an amazing ability to get her passion and caring energy across to others without actually needing to be in the same room with them. Talk about multiplication; think how many more people we can help. That same weekend, Lee, the Queen of Marketing, as well as the Queen of So Much Else, shared new ways to market our services. Again, helping us reach more people.

Collaboration is so much more effective than competition. If Susan in Philadelphia has a client who has training needs for his employees in Chicago, she will probably call me, Gina, Barbara or Lauri, and hire one of us to do it for her. I might call Lauri and ask her to help me with a proposal I'm putting together. Maybe some of us will get together and put on a joint presentation. We all know we can deliver the same message with the same passion and in-depth knowledge. We trust each other with our most precious business asset: our clients.

I believe everyone in the world has the same job: we are here to love each other. You can be Oprah Winfrey and everyone can see how you contribute, or you can be me, and maybe just a few people will know of my contributions. But that doesn't mean they aren't there.

I don't stress out anymore about not having "enough" time or money to make a difference in the world. I know that I don't need to sacrifice myself to others in order to be a good person. And I certainly don't need others to sacrifice for me in order to have what I want.

Whatever I do—facilitate, coach, work with dogs, live a green life—there are two things I must ask myself. First: does this serve the earth and its creatures? Does it make the world a better place? And second: Does this feed my heart? Does it make me happy? I've learned that I must answer "yes" to both. If I do, I know that this is what I am meant to do with my life.

Can't get any bigger than that.

Only One Shopping Day Left Until Tomorrow: *Lauri*

My professional life began as a teacher, and I loved being a mom. Helping children grow and develop has been a passion of mine for as long as I can remember. Then later when I became a businesswoman I found I loved the business world, too. But it wasn't until I learned about Rainbows For All Children that I discovered I could satisfy both of my passions at once.

Rainbows for All Children (www.rainbows.org) is an international charity that supports children going through the grieving process. Their grief could be over the death of a parent or other family member, grief over parental divorce, grief when a parent or sibling is incarcerated, or grief from any kind of disaster. Rainbows for All Children sent money and counselors to New Orleans to help the children after Hurricane Katrina. Rainbows for All Children was also there for young adults who were impacted by the shootings at Virginia Tech.

Rainbows for All Children' grief support programs have helped over two million children since they were founded in 1983. They are based in Chicago, but I had never heard of them until I got married. My husband Randy's best friend is married to Suzy Yehl Marta, the founder of Rainbows for All Children. Random chance? I don't think so. It's divine intervention, yet again.

Suzy is one of those charismatic people whose passion is so contagious that few people are immune to its sweeping force. As soon as I met her and learned about Rainbows for All Children, I was hooked. As a volunteer for Rainbows for All Children I could help children, use my sales skills by fundraising, and capitalize on my managerial talents by organizing charitable events. All at the same time!

Rainbows for All Children came along at a perfect time in my life. I had been working hard for as far back as I could remember, and had now achieved some success and stability. I had a beautiful home, a loving husband, my children were now adults, and had as many "things" as I needed. Now it was time to use what I'd learned and what I'd gained for the greater good. It was time to feed my soul.

I told the girls about Rainbows for All Children during a girls' weekend at Susan's beach house on the Jersey shore—the same weekend we met Mario and sang karaoke. See? We're not just fun and games!

I must have sounded nearly as passionate as Suzy, because I found it easy to convince my friends. "Let's donate as a group," I suggested. "If we each donated only $167, we could give $1,000 and be considered Angel Donors." And so we did. I sent all six checks along with a letter to Suzy, and signed it from all of us. I told her about the Bad Girls—who we were individually and how we had grown into a group of women dedicated to using our training skills to help people be all they could be. I closed by asking her what else we could do to help Rainbows for All Children. Could she use our facilitating expertise in some way? Could we train her volunteers?

I guess she liked the letter, because she wrote back almost immediately with an exciting proposal. "I've wanted to create a Women's Board supporting Rainbows for All Children for a long time," she wrote. "You sound like the perfect people to start it up. Would you be willing?"

What a silly question. Of course we were willing! The six of us, along with a few others who Suzy recommended, originated the Women's Board. The first thing we did was draft a mission statement. We tried to make it memorable and meaningful; our mission was to "Have Fun, Make Money, and Do Good." It wasn't the most profound and elegantly written mission statement, but it did define who we were and what we wanted to accomplish. The two events our board initiated are based on the Bad Girls' own particular ideas of fun. I'm an art lover and because of my friendship with Barbara and the girls, I'd become somewhat of a 'wine snob.' Barbara and I thought it would be a hoot if we could combine those two elements, so we planned and organized Rainbows for All Children' first fundraiser, a wine-and-art-auction we called "Canvases and Corks." It wasn't hard to convince our newly-minted board that this event would fulfill our mission of "having fun, making money, and doing good." *Canvases and Corks* is an annual gala now in its sixth year. Several years ago Lee was the auctioneer and moderator of the event. Everyone wants her back again because when Lee is on stage, she can get anyone to do anything. She's magic and amazing and gorgeous and you can't take your eyes off her.

Of course, it's not always total fun; there's a lot of hard work that goes into running an affair like this. One year I thought it would be fun to make baskets for a raffle, and sell hand-painted lighted wine bottles. Only I didn't arrange for artists to paint the bottles; I thought we—the Women's Board, which at that time was expanding—could paint them. Of course, none of us were artists, a fact that I didn't think much about, until those empty bottles were in front of us.

"Are you kidding me?" said Gina, when she showed up at the bottle-painting party and saw 100 empty wine bottles waiting. I tried to sell it as an adventure, but it wasn't until everyone had a few glasses of wine that they were able to see it that way. Gina, Nicki and Barbara became known as the "glitter girls" because we decided that glitter would be the final Bad Girls touch to our Women's Board fund-raising project. We had a blast and our wine bottles were a huge success.

This year the Women's Board has a new event, also based on what I like to do for fun—shopping! It's called "The Power of the Purse: a Ladies' Luncheon and Shopping Experience." We're having purse raffles and a variety of shopping treats; ladies can buy purses, lingerie, shoes, and jewelry from local merchants who have donated a portion of their profits to Rainbows for All Children. We're billing it as a "Day of Indulgence."

Naturally the girls have teased me about this event, because my love for shopping has become one of our running jokes. But I think pairing what makes you happy with what makes you proud is a good idea. Service and fun together is an unbeatable combination.

I think pairing what makes you happy with what makes you proud is a good idea. Service and fun together is an unbeatable combination.

Since its inception, the Rainbow Women's Board has grown to 27 members and so far we've raised over $500,000 to help grieving children. And this accomplishment all grew out of one of our fun-filled girls' weekends and a $167 individual donation.

The Best Gift: *Gina*

Lauri is right. When you do what makes you happy, it makes other people happy, too. I love to teach, although I never wanted to be a regular school teacher who taught reading and math and other academics. What I love to teach are practical life skills and how to be nice to one another. There's a word for that—it's called manners.

Manners are at the heart of all the training I do, whether it's leadership training or a course on how to hire and fire employees. If you don't treat people with courtesy, you won't be much of a leader!

Manners are so much more than learning which fork to use, how to address your elders, or the etiquette of email. Manners are the grease that makes communication possible. Without manners society couldn't function. But with our children today, manners have taken a back seat to academics as a way to get ahead. I think this is a mistake.

It sounds funny to say that I have a passion for good manners; it makes me sound like Emily Post, or some prune-lipped skinny spinster. And you know, I'm a bosomy Italian woman with a big voice, and have been known to wear racy t-shirts while strutting my stuff down the street. I don't think Emily Post ever did that.

Nevertheless, I'm big on good manners. They are so important to me that I volunteer a significant portion of my free time teaching manners to others besides my clients. I developed a course for children called *Everyday Manners*, which I teach at my son's school and for the local Girl Scout troops. I also volunteer my time to teach manners to the winner of the Miss Illinois pageant, our state's entry to the Miss America program. Not that she doesn't already have good manners, but you'd be surprised how much a young woman needs to know about how to get along with numerous people of diverse outlooks. And how to do it under stress, too.

Besides teaching manners, I also volunteer a year's worth of life coaching to each year's Miss Illinois. I'm one of a team of people who prepare her for the Miss America pageant, held every January. Someone helps her with interviewing skills, someone else coaches her on her fashion style, and another works with her on her particular talent. I do the "psychological" coaching, helping her move forward in any arena she feels is lacking. Perhaps she wants to work on her confidence, or be clear about her goals, or learn how to show genuine emotion without weeping all over the stage. These young women are outstanding, and I feel so honored to work with them. It doesn't matter to me whether they win the title of Miss America or not. What does matter is that they go on to live productive and happy lives, and to know that I made a small contribution to their success.

I got the other Bad Girls involved in the Miss Illinois pageant, too. For several years, we donated funds to purchase the beautiful gold-inlaid wooden box that holds the new Miss Illinois' crown. Recognition for our contribution appears in the annual pageant memory book, which is important to us, not because we want to toot our own horn, but because we want to show how women can support other women.

We support each other as if we are family, because we *are* family now. We love each other's husbands, kids, brothers, sisters, and parents. One night my mother had a gig at a cabaret in Chicago, and all six of the Bad Girls turned out for her first night—even Lee from Florida and Susan from Philadelphia. The girls love my mom. She is the original Bad Girl. I know the first time I put on my Bad Girls t-shirt and sang in that conference talent show, I had to channel my mother the nightclub singer. Otherwise I don't know how I would have pulled it off. My mom is the bravest woman I know.

The night we were all there, Mom sang with Mario Lanza's son, Victor. He's been a friend of my mom's for nearly forty years, and they've sung together often on the entertainment circuit. He looks just like his dad, and I think his voice is just as good, too.

Glittered Up with Star Quality

He took a big liking to Lee, flirted with her all night. It was pretty funny because he's about a foot shorter than she is.

When Mom sang *How Come You Do Me Like You Do, Do, Do,* which is a very sultry song, Victor made lovey-dovey faces at Lee, and she made them right back. What a hoot.

My mother has also entertained at some of our Rainbow events. She's always a hit, all glittered up with that star quality she has. She's in her seventies now, but she's still belting those cabaret songs out like she's in her thirties.

The Bad Girls also support each other by contributing to each other's pet charities. Together we have an even bigger effect. Lauri got us all to volunteer for her favorite charity Rainbows for All Children, and it's been an exciting ride. Lauri has so many ideas—not all of them workable, but most of them interesting. "Interesting" is the most charitable way to describe my artistic efforts in painting those wine bottles. I bet the people who charitably purchased my bottles wondered why Rainbows for All Children let two-year-olds paint them. Actually, two-year-olds probably would have done a better job. Although after a while I got pretty good with the glitter.

Maybe the bottle-painting event was the reason I was so suspicious when Lauri told me she wanted to organize a dinner for the six of us to celebrate my 50th birthday. Whenever Lauri gets to organize anything, it sort of takes on a life of its own. "I don't want an adventure," I said. "Let's just have a nice dinner together."

"Oh, of course," she said. "Just a nice dinner." But there was something about her innocent voice …

On the night of the dinner, the other five Bad Girls picked me up, and took me to a beautiful French restaurant called *Café La Cave* in Des Plaines, IL. We had a lovely martini at the bar, made just the way we like them, and I suggested we order some appetizers, when Lauri said, "Oh, I forgot to tell you we need to do something first. We need to go to the hotel across the street; they're having an art auction. Let's see if we can pick up some good buys on art pieces for *Canvases and Corks*."

"Right now?" I said.

"Yeah, it's just across the street," she said. "It's a great opportunity to get some good art for the Rainbows for All Children event. It'll only take fifteen minutes, really. Greater good, Gina, greater good! We can come right back for dinner, I promise."

The other girls seemed to agree with Lauri, so although I was having a fabulous time where we were, I reluctantly said okay. Lauri can get me to do nearly anything when she starts up on the greater good. I told the bartender we'd be back in half an hour, and don't forget how to make our blue-cheese olive stuffed martinis!

We walked across the street to the hotel, and before anyone could stop me I went up to the reader board that lists the events being held. "Hey, there's no art auction listed," I said. "Are we in the wrong hotel? Or is this another adventure? We're going to miss our reservations. I want to go back to the restaurant. I'm gonna kill you guys!"

I think it was Barbara who quickly said, "No, it's not going to be posted; it's a private event. I know the name of the room, so let's just go there." Barbara thinks well on her feet.

You can donate money, volunteer your services, and give in so many ways to others, and all of them make you feel great. But do you know one of the best gifts you can give? It's when you let others give to you.

Now, I'm an old hotel-person, so I knew that even private events are listed on the reader board, but it's hard to argue with Barbara when she uses her calm authoritarian voice. You just naturally believe her. So they led me down a hallway to the banquet rooms. But when we got there, the banquet doors were closed; it was obviously a private function. This was confirmed when a bartender came down the hall and went into the room. I caught a glimpse of a bunch of people milling around.

"This is no art auction," I said. "It's a private party, we can't butt in here. It's bad manners!" Like I said, I'm big on good manners. There was no way I was going in that room.

Except that the girls wouldn't let me leave. All talking at once, they told me I was wrong; it really was an auction, just not a formal one. We didn't have to stay long. If I felt uncomfortable, we would leave right away. All the time they were talking, they were inching me closer and closer to the door, until they finally got me inside the room.

And that's when the place erupted with cheers. The milling people weren't strangers; I knew everyone in that room, because they were there to honor my birthday. My husband had planned the whole thing—including getting the Bad Girls to get me there without spoiling the surprise. In addition to my entire family, Guy had invited fifty—fifty to match my age—of the most fabulous women in my life. They all gave speeches. It was one of the sweetest evenings of my life.

You can donate money, volunteer your services, and give in so many ways to others, and all of them make you feel great. But do you know one of the best gifts you can give? It's when you let others give to you.

Home to My Sistahs: *Susan*

Having lived all over the world, from Oklahoma to Amsterdam to Chicago to Philadelphia, I don't have much of an accent. I sound like I'm from everywhere. But when I married Jack, I began to pick up his accent, which is pure Jersey. (Or as he would say, "Joisey.") Jack started calling my Bad Girl friends the "Sistahs." I thought it sounded cute, and I had often mentioned that the Bad Girls were as close as sisters; so I started calling us that, too. Soon we were all doing it.

I thought it was just Jack's accent that made "sister" sound like "sistah," but I have since learned that "sistah" has a deeper meaning than just biological female siblings.

I've been told that "sistah" or "sista" was originally a term that African-American women used with each other, to express their solidarity. It is commonly used to mean a female friend who is as close as family who you can always count on and can always count on you. It is a heart connection that is based on mutual love and respect. A "sistah" is someone who will always have your back, no matter what.

Well, how perfect is that! I cannot think of a better definition for the Bad Girls. Some families you are born into, and there are some that you choose. The Bad Girls are the second kind of family. We truly are sistahs.

This was brought forcibly home to me on July 3, 2009 when I was in a severe car accident. I was driving alone, happily singing along with the radio, when another car veered out of control and hit me nearly head-on, then swung around to hit me again on the driver's side. My car was so badly totaled that the tow truck driver who later towed the car away was stunned when he was told I was not dead. "Nah, she's gotta be dead," he claimed.

I was close to dead. My head hit the glass in the driver's window, which broke into long lethal splinters, one of which stabbed into a vein on the side of my head. Blood spurted out like water out of a leaky garden hose.

Because the car was smashed—there was only one foot between the back of the front seat and the dashboard—I could not get out of the car myself. My legs were pinned. Smoke billowed out of the dash, and the whole car was hot. I was still conscious, and my only thought was that my car was going to explode with me inside it. I wasn't really aware of how much blood was pouring out the side of my head. I began to yell and scream for help.

Two men showed up by the window. They started to debate what they should do. Should they move me or not? How badly hurt was I? Where's all that blood coming from? Should they wait for the ambulance and the cops? What if the car exploded before they got there?

Another man came up, a big guy with a ponytail and a bunch of tattoos. He looked like a biker. Without any hesitation he leaned into the car and looked right into my terrified eyes. "Put your arms around my neck and I'll pull you out," he said. Then he and one of the other guys lifted me through the window, and laid me gently on the ground. I was looking up at him when I blacked out.

When I came to I was lying on a stretcher, while the paramedics prepared to lift me into the ambulance. I couldn't see my biker guy anywhere, and I became agitated. I had to thank him! "Where's the biker guy? Where's my angel?" I said over and over.

They finally found him, and he came over to me. I reached my hand up to touch his face. "Bless you. God bless you," I muttered, right before I blacked out again.

That was the last time I saw him. Later Jack tried to get his name, so we could thank him, but he told the police he didn't want to be contacted. But I will never, ever forget him. Angels don't just wear wings and white robes. They also wear black leather and tattoos.

The car didn't explode, and I didn't die. However, the car went to the junk yard and I spent months and months in rehab. I had lost a great deal of blood, and suffered a brain injury.

One of the first people Jack called after the accident was Barbara. Barbara told me later it was a miracle they were able to understand each other, because they were both crying so hard. Barbara was still crying when she called the others. Then they cried. But after the crying, their next reaction was to get on a plane to visit us where we now lived in Pennsylvania. They were stopped by Jack and the doctors, who told them not to come because people with traumatic brain injuries need lots of quiet to begin healing. Each of my sistahs told me later that the hardest thing about my accident for them was not being able to touch me, look into my eyes, and hear my voice.

But during those first weeks when I wasn't allowed visitors, my sistahs were constantly in touch with me through prayer. I could *feel* them praying.

Angels don't just wear wings and white robes. They also wear black leather and tattoos.

In practical terms, Jack and Barbara talked a couple of times a week on the phone, and Jack sent out long status emails to everyone every other day. I missed them and they missed me, but we made it through.

After a few months, the sistahs really began agitating to come to Pennsylvania. We could talk on the phone by this time, and "We want to see you," was the constant refrain. I understood completely, because I felt the same way; I wanted to see them, too. The sentence that kept coming up for me was, "I want to go home to my sistahs."

I even had dreams in which this sentence figured prominently.

I told Jack, "I don't want the Bad Girls to come here. I want to go home to see them." Home to me meant Chicago, where we met and the Bad Girls began.

I don't think my doctors were happy with the idea of me going across the country "just to see my girlfriends," but that's because they didn't understand what sistah-hood meant. Thankfully Jack does understand, so he and I went to stay with Barbara and Rick, and the rest of the Bad Girls came for a day while Jack, Rick, Lauri's husband Randy and Gina's husband Guy went to a Cubs-Phillies game and then out for beers or something—whatever guys do when they get together. They had become friends, too, through us.

We just hung out together all day, talking about our lives, singing a little, making plans for "next time." I couldn't do much because I was often dizzy, and had to sleep a lot. It didn't matter, to them or to me. I knew I didn't have to put on any appearances. We just wanted to be together. I knew by then that I could easily have died, that in fact it was a miracle I didn't. I once heard a quote about dying that explained it as, "concentrating your mind wonderfully." This is true. When you come close to death, it becomes so clear what is really important—the people you love. Yes, I know there is nothing new about this insight. We pay lip-service to it. But we don't always pay it heart-service. Unless you have sistahs like mine.

During one of my little naps, while I lay drowsily on Barbara's bed, I could hear the Bad Girls in the kitchen below, making dinner. They were singing as they worked, one of our favorites, an old Dionne Warwick hit from the eighties, *"That's What Friends are For."*

"Keep smiling, keep shinin', knowing you can always count on me, for sure ... That's what friends are for. For good times and bad times, I'll be on your side forever more, That's what friends are for."

I felt so blessed and grateful to God or Spirit or the Universe to have been saved and given my life. I would no longer take life for granted. I had a second chance to fulfill my purpose, to find the reason I was born.

I always wanted to be a giver, not a taker. But listening to my sistahs sing I realized that it's not enough to give to others with grace. You have to learn to take with grace, too. Sometimes you must allow others to fill you up.

Long before my accident, when we first began talking about writing a book, I was the first one pushing the idea. I said, "You know, we're not going to live forever. What can we leave behind about the magic we've created between us? How can our experiences help the next generation of women? How can we be a force for good?"

I want other women—and men—to be inspired by our connection and to know that they can create the same for themselves. You can tell yourself different stories and clear the blockages that get in your way. You can move forward toward your dreams. You can. All you need is some sistahs to bring you home.

What can we leave behind about the magic we've created between us? How can our experiences help the next generation of women? How can we be a force for good?

There's a reason you are here. There's a reason others are in your life. This reason is always the same: it's to help and love one another. Every spiritual leader the world has ever known has said this. That is because it is true.

Spit Pact Gratitude: *Barbara*

The Law of Attraction sounds really good, doesn't it? Focus on the good and you'll attract it into your life. Easy-peasey, no problem-o. Right?

But one of the difficulties many of us run into is that "focus on the good" is kind of vague. What does that really mean, in practical, down-to-earth stuff that you can *do*? That's not as easy.

We were discussing this challenge during one of our girls' weekends, when I had a good idea. (I love it when that happens!) I suggested that in addition to looking for the positive everywhere, we might try to focus our "attraction beam" on our significant others. We would consciously notice what was good about them. We would notice if they were acting kindly, being generous, told a funny joke, or if they looked particularly nice—and we'd also *tell* them what we noticed. We'd actively look for ways to compliment them, in other words. But—and this is an important but—we wouldn't tell our significant others what we were doing. It would be a Spit Pact between the six of us.

Everyone loved this idea. We agreed that we'd report back to each other via group emails, so we could actually track how this practical application of the Law of Attraction was working.

Sometimes the simple ideas are the great ones. The following

Monday the emails started to fly. They've been flying steadily since.

To: The Bad Girls
From: Barbara
This morning I overheard Rick on the phone with his brother helping him solve a business challenge that he was having. I said, "You are such a good friend and confidant to your brother, he is lucky to have you!" He was so cute. His shoulders went back and he had this silly smile on his face. He said, "Thanks for sharing that with me. I really appreciate it."

To: The Bad Girls
From: Gina
Since Guy was made Fire Chief, I have to say that his new dress uniform is the sexiest thing I've ever seen. You know me, I'm kind of modest so I've kept this thought to myself. But then I thought, next time he wears it I'll tell him how sexy he looks. So last week Guy put on his uniform for a special event. Oh my God, I got weak at the knees. I put my hands on his shoulders and said, "You know, I just want to work you over for a few minutes, you sexy thing." He got the cutest look on his face. I can't really describe it. But all he said was, "Okay." Just that, "okay," in that monotone he uses when he can't think of what to say. I'll leave the rest of this story to your imagination.

To: The Bad Girls
From: Barbara
With this horrible economy, we're going through a very difficult

time financially right now. It's so easy to fall into negative thinking. The other day we were standing in the kitchen talking about how we were going to juggle everything—what to spend, what to sell, what to do. Rick was explaining a particularly difficult tactic he thought might work, when I reached for his hand and said, "I just want you to know how much I appreciate the time, effort and skill you have. I know that we will make it through this because of you." His eyebrows shot up and he didn't say anything for a minute. Then he came over and gave me a great big hug. "Thank you so much," he said. The anxiety in his voice was gone.

To: The Bad Girls

From: Susan

Jack got home from a business trip last night. When he walked in the door he just looked so handsome in his suit. I love the way he looks in starched shirts (weird, maybe, but it's just my thing). I said, "Oooh, honey, you look so handsome. I LOVE you in that shirt!" He just smiled and said, "Oh, really." Then he went upstairs, took off his suit but kept that shirt on with his jeans. I went crazy when he came back downstairs. Needless to say, he had on another starched shirt today! ☺

When you focus on the good, you attract it into your life. These emails proved this to be so true. Not only did our SOs feel good, so did we.

Soon our emails started to note the compliments coming back to us. Rick isn't the type to notice what I'm wearing or how I look. Compliments are not really his thing; he's more of a "show it not talk it" kind of guy. But one day not long after we began our experiment, he walked up to me and gave me a hug, saying, "You look great in that dress." I could hardly wait to email the girls and tell them!

Another thing that happened as a result of our SOs feeling good about themselves, is that they passed that positive focus on to others—their kids, their clients or co-workers, the checkers at the grocery store, the many people they met during the course of their regular day out and about. They noticed the nice things that people said and did, and thanked them for it.

And like a stone making ripples in a pond, I'd bet a lot of money that those people were nicer to the people *they* met. "Pay It Forward" really works.

Lee and I took this idea one step further during a trip we took to New York City. Lee brought a bunch of little smiley-face pins with her that were printed with the message, "I really appreciate what you do." She wanted to give these pins to the various people we met in New York.

"You know what a bad rap New Yorkers get," she explained. "They're supposed to be so blunt and impolite, but I don't think that's really true. I think people are *expecting* New Yorkers to be rude and abrupt, so guess what kind of people they draw toward them? I think if we expect New Yorkers to be helpful and courteous, and we tell them so when they are, we'll have a great time."

She was so right! We gave Lee's little buttons to a porter at the airport, taxi drivers, waiters and waitresses, the usher at the theatre, the concierge at the hotel, and even a woman we met riding in the elevator with us. Our main criterion was that they were helpful and courteous, although friendly was good, too. The only thing the woman in the elevator did was smile and wish us "good morning" when we got on.

It sounds kind of hokey, right? Almost like hippies handing out flowers to total strangers during the sixties? Wrong, wrong, wrong! People loved it. They loved it because our appreciation was real, not phony. It was based on us noticing the good about them that was actually there.

We gave our button to a server wearing a crazy tie, mismatched shoes and a happy voice that made us feel happy, too. As we paid our check, we handed him the button and said, "We really want to thank you for being such a great server." A grin spread across his face and he pinned the button on his shirt. He kissed us both and thanked us. Then he went over to his next table and said, "Look what I just got!" Everyone at the table laughed and agreed that he was a great server. The next night we stopped by that same restaurant for a drink on the way back to the hotel, and there was our server, still showing off his button and sharing the story about the nice ladies who gave it to him.

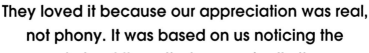

They loved it because our appreciation was real, not phony. It was based on us noticing the good about them that was actually there.

One morning we went to a diner that you had to wait a really long time to get in because it was famous both for its food and the friendliness of the host. Even though you had to wait a long time, you didn't care because he was so nice and made it fun to wait. After breakfast, Lee went up to him and said, in a very serious tone, "Excuse me, could we speak to you for just a minute?"

"Certainly," he said, matching her tone. Lee said, "We just so appreciate how great you made us feel this morning and we want you to have this button." She handed it to him like it was the Nobel Prize. Lee and her dramatic flair!

He took the button and stared at it in his hand. "Thank you," he said. And I'm not kidding, he had tears in his eyes.

All energy we expend has a boomerang effect. When you give out positive energy, it will surround you and everyone around you, causing all of you to become more positive, which again causes more positive energy to grow. The opposite is also true—negative energy begets more negativity. Our little experiment is not difficult. Try it yourself on your significant other and see what happens.

Our Spit Pact is still in place, or it was until we wrote about it in this book. None of our significant others knew about the experiment until now, although I think Rick suspected. One day while having coffee in bed I turned to Rick and said, "I love hearing your voice in the morning. It starts my day off right."

"I don't know where all this is coming from," he said. "But I really love it." I just smiled. He added, "You're not going to tell me, are you?"

"No, I'm not," I said, and kissed him.

Lee: *We're All Somebody*

In the fall of 2009 I had back surgery. I've had a number of medical challenges in my life, and I have always tried to handle them with positive energy and encouraging self-talk. Something good will come of this, I say. The pain and discomfort will pass.

This does work, but it works even better when you combine it with loving energy from other people. We don't like to think of ourselves—at least I don't—as being needy. But that's just ego talking. All of us are needy sometimes. And when we are, it's good to have people who can fill our needs with love.

We planned a girls' weekend in Chicago that November, when we'd be together at our annual *Canvases and Corks* event for Rainbows for All Children. But because of my back pain and the surgery being scheduled just a few days afterwards, I could not go. I was disappointed, and so were the girls. "Oh no, Lee," said Barbara. "Since your big birthday is coming up in January, we were going to throw you a surprise birthday party." Well, that made me even more disappointed. On the day of my should-be party, I pictured them laughing, playing how-you-doin', reading angel cards, singing and dancing, drinking those silly martinis, and I have to admit I felt pretty down, no matter how many self-talks I gave myself.

Until my phone rang that evening. It was them—all of them together on the phone at once, plus their spouses. They told me about the new plan they'd made. Since I was unable to come to Chicago in November, they decided to come to Florida in January to celebrate my actual birthday with me. Plus, we would celebrate my recovery from back pain, which had been cramping my party style for much too long. "Now remember," they said right before we hung up the phone, "Just before you go under the anesthetic, when you're really high and feeling great, think about us. Because we'll be thinking about you."

I remembered, and did just that. Right after the nurse gave

me the shot that made everything feel soooo good, there they were—Barbara, Lauri, Susan, Nicki and Gina. I saw, as clearly as I've seen anything, their faces looking down at me and smiling. Their faces were full of love. Love for me. Right then I knew that everything was going to be all right.

It was. By the time January 2010 and my birthday rolled around, I felt pretty darn good. Every day I felt stronger and more flexible. I looked forward to dancing my shoes off at the girls' weekend. I felt young and light and ready for whatever came next.

Oh, what a glorious weekend it was, all my best friends hanging out at my house. We did all the things we always do. I'd laid in a supply of vodka and vermouth, blue cheese olives, and we kicked off the celebration with our signature martinis. The girls brought me a birthday present, a pink teddy bear wearing a feathery pink frou-frou hat and a string of pearls, who we named Lee-Lee-Belle. We linked arms (Lee-Lee-Belle needed some help) and sang *That's What Friends are For*—off key as usual—while we danced a swaying snake-dance through the kitchen. Lauri made incredible caviar canapés, which disappeared with remarkable speed. I think Gina ate six. We chose angel cards; I drew Friendship. How perfect was that? Of course, angel cards are always perfect—what else would you expect from angels? And we laughed so hard and talked so much the walls started to shake. Okay, I may be exaggerating just a little.

Doing the things we always do connects us to the foundation of our friendship. It reminds us of who we are and why we came together. But that doesn't mean we let ourselves stagnate; we make it a point each time to kick it up another notch by learning or trying something new, something different, something better.

This weekend was especially ripe with new ideas. We were in the process of writing this book, and we all knew we were on the verge of taking "The Bad Girls" out into the world. How should we present ourselves? Bad Girls or Do-Gooders? Sistahs or Fun-Lovers? Light Workers or Karaoke singers? Maybe all of the above? Above all, how do we offer what we know to be true and good, and make a positive difference in the world?

Barbara's answer was through her work with *The Enrichment Process™*. It had been evolving over the past year; she'd been working hard to combine a spiritual dimension with the psychological techniques. "You're gonna love this," she told us. "Regardless of what our religious beliefs are, we are connected to a Source. There's a layer between us as human beings and the universe, whether we call it God, or angels, or Higher Power, or whatever. We're guided all day by this higher power, this knowing. I want to consciously bring this knowing into each process to make it deeper and even stronger."

We did love it, just like Barbara knew we would. We spent a day processing each other, through Barbara's skillful direction tapping into the higher knowing we all have. This is Barbara's gift to the world. It's up to us to help her get it out there.

Later that evening Gina brought up the idea of creating a website for the book, and starting a blog. If a blog about following the recipes in *The French Chef* could result in a movie as good as *Julie and Julia*, then surely we could do the same. "What about helping women form 'Bad Girls circles'?" asked Susan. "Or maybe a Facebook group?" Lauri mused aloud about sponsorships and promotions, and then asked, "How can we motivate women in the business world to allow themselves to be vulnerable and still keep the respect they need to succeed?" Nicki batted out an "elevator speech" for us to use at networking events. Nicki, who used to believe she couldn't write at all! I'm so glad she gave up that belief.

So many ideas—where to start?

Then Susan, our spiritual guide, chimed in. "I don't want to push," she said. "I don't think we need to. I want to let go and let the book and our next projects just evolve. I want us to be guided by Spirit. Instead of trying to force it, trying to do all these things at once, we need to listen to our angels. Let the energy pull us toward where we're meant to go. After all, isn't that what we're all about?"

Indeed. You just have to love Susan.

How can we motivate women in the business world to allow themselves to be vulnerable and still keep the respect they need to succeed?

I'd been silent through most of the discussion, because until Susan spoke I hadn't been sure about my future vision for the Bad Girls. But suddenly I knew.

"My spirit is really stirred about this and I think it's something we have to do," I said. "I have no idea what it's going to look like, and I don't think we need to know yet. But I do know there is something big coming."

"My whole career has been about helping people reach, grow, and be the best they can be. I've managed major corporations and helped their people, especially women, achieve their goals.

I'm a hard-working professional motivational speaker, continually speaking about personal growth topics. Now I'm joining my experience with my best friends, to achieve our mission of helping people see the beauty within themselves. It's all about showing them how to change the bad stories they tell themselves to good ones."

"I remember when I was a little girl, I felt like nobody. My biggest desire was to be somebody. I want to provide people with what I never had provided to me—I want them to know that they already are somebody."

When you've said what you have to say, the best thing to do then is dance. That's one way to make it real. I turned up the music, swung my hips and waved my arms as if I was thirty again (I was!). I unbuttoned my candy-pink shirt to show some cleavage. Lauri, bright as sunshine in yellow sweats, threw her arms around my middle and we sashayed together across the floor in a tango never seen before (or since). Then Barbara in her red sweater and black pants dipped and slid across the floor; Nicki, in baggy grey sweats, and Gina, in a University of Illinois hoodie, did some John Travolta moves; and finally, Susan, in her pink flannel jammies tried to do the Michael Jackson moonwalk.

A new song came on. "Goody!" we yelled, and moved our butts to *"Second That Emotion"*, by Diana Ross and the Supremes. Hey, we *are* Diana Ross and the Supremes, without the spangles.

No, we're just the Bad Girls, doing our thing.

At Rainbows for All Children Canvases and Corks *Gala*

△

SEVEN

We've Only Just Begun

$\mathcal{I}$t's six o'clock in the morning—*Monday* morning. The six of us are sitting around a plastic table in a restaurant/lounge in the Chicago airport. We're drinking espresso, very dark and strong. We've just finished a girls' weekend at Lauri's house, including a wildly successful Ladies Luncheon Experience for Rainbows for All Children. Now we're off to another conference which starts that evening in Los Angeles. There are some good speakers—we know this for sure because Susan is one of them—and we're looking forward to learning some new things.

Well, we will be looking forward in a little while, maybe not now. It's six in the morning, after all. It was the only time we could get a non-stop out of Chicago that would get us to LA in time. We're tired because we don't always get enough sleep when we get together. We're like little kids who don't want to go to bed; we might miss something!

Gina starts humming *We've Only Just Begun*. Nicki joins in, only she substitutes words ("we've only just begun … to wink") which is dumb but makes us all giggle anyway. Lee points out a handsome man walking by. Barbara says, "Lee! Don't you wink too!" and Lee swears she isn't. Susan has made changes to her speech

193

and she tries it out on us. Her hands float and weave through the air as she talks. Lauri says, "Ooh, what about this?" and makes a suggestion. Susan eagerly agrees, scribbling notes. Soon we're all making comments, suggestions, atta-girls, high fives, and the energy shifts from "My god why are we up so damn early?" to "It's fun at six in the morning!"

People walking by smile at us. A teenage boy gives us a thumbs-up. A woman stops at our table and says, "Where are you girls going? Wherever it is, I want to go with you!"

Here we go again, the Bad Girls lightening up the world, in little tiny ways. It's our mission, and we have accepted it. No, we've embraced it.

We hope you will join us!

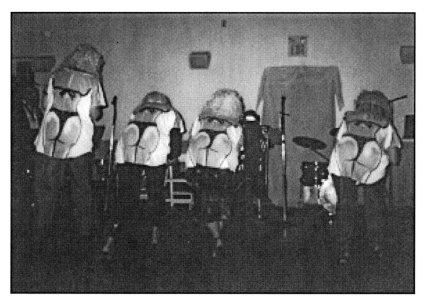

The End!

EIGHT

MEET THE GIRLS

Barbara

A generous leader who inspires and supports all six girlfriends. Follow her transition from a suburban Chicago boutique owner to the president of a training and consulting business. Understand as she takes a big risk and steps up and follows her heart and instincts in spite of an unsettled life and the advice of others. As a recognized author and founder of Enrichment Technologies, Barbara's passion and dedication for showing others how to tap into their own strength and wisdom to make positive changes in their lives becomes her proudest professional accomplishment. Her passion for the technology also becomes the foundation for all the changes that the women in this story were able to make.

Lauri

The enthusiastic adventurer who makes things happen and gets things done. She is filled with ideas and energizes (as well as exhausts) the girls with her "go-for-it" emotion and energy. Follow her transformation from English schoolteacher to a business writing consultant to ultimately a recognized business consultant for Fortune 100 companies in the automotive industry. Share her struggles with divorce and religious beliefs. Learn of her passionate philanthropic devotion to helping children who struggle with the grief of losing a parent to death, divorce, incarceration or military deployment.

Susan

The loving, warm-hearted spiritual rock who is dedicated to lifelong learning and making a positive difference in the world. Follow her as she wins a scholarship to Oxford and leaves her small conservative Oklahoma town to learn the meaning of independence and freedom of thought. Read about her life-threatening automobile accident and how the spirit of friendship pulled her through to a safe recovery. Susan is recognized, awarded and acclaimed by Fortune 100 companies for her entrepreneurial business success in leadership development and team building.

Gina

The devoted and dedicated mother and wife of a Chicago fire chief, this sassy Italian gal shares her fondest experiences of overcoming her fear-based childhood beliefs to becoming enormously successful in the field of hotel management, training, consulting and client coaching. Understand how Gina's religion and close-knit Italian family define and influence her values and relationships. Share her passion for helping others find and develop their own life's path with grace and courage through the philanthropic work she does with local Chicago area schools and the Miss Illinois Scholarship Association.

Lee

The chic, sophisticated and humorous storyteller who is a trailblazer and mentor for hundreds of women executives. Her enthusiasm, marketing expertise and passion are contagious and have contributed to her success in life and business. Besides owning a business development firm and her own training company, Lee is in demand as a motivational speaker who inspires as well as entertains. Known as "Jackie-O" by the girls for her style and wisdom, learn how Lee's strength, positive attitude, humor and courage helped her face difficult personal and professional transitions with substance and style.

Nicki:

The self-described "late bloomer" and youngest of the six girls. Follow Nicki as she evolves from a belief that she is a poor student to her courageous decision to attend college in her adulthood. Watch and validate her accomplishments as she turns into a super student and is awarded with superior grades and teacher's recognition. Join in her story of a courageous spirit and determination to never give up. Laugh at her story as the "other Italian" of the group as she experiences drinking "big girl martinis" at her first business conference. Follow her as she learns project management, finds business success in starting her own Organizational Development and Training business, and delivers highly-rated workshops in Leadership, Process Improvement and Customer Service.

For more in-depth professional information on the background and careers of these women, please go to www.SixFiguresBook.com

For more information on "Six Figures" workshops, go to www.SixFiguresWorkshops.com

Cheers!

NINE

RECIPES

The Perfect Six Figures Martini

Martini glasses in the freezer – super chilled

Queen size olives stuffed with blue cheese —
an olive stuffer and fresh blue cheese makes it perfect

4 to 5 ounces of Ketel One Citroen Vodka per
drink (Absolute works well too) coming straight
from the freezer

1 ounce Martini and Rossi Dry Vermouth – refrigerated

1 martini shaker filled with ice stored in the freezer

*The key to a wonderful **Six Figures Martini** is to have everything frozen or super chilled. Add your vodka to martini shaker, then add vermouth and store in freezer until ready to pour then shake vigorously (great exercise), place olive in glass and pour over. Always do a positive toast to all that are enjoying your special time together. Most importantly, ENJOY!*

Jackie O's Cosmo

1 martini glass chilling in the freezer

3 ounces of Ketel One Citroen or Absolute Citroen Vodka

1 ounce of Cranberry Juice

1 ounce of Triple Sec

½ Lemon

1 martini shaker (separate from the other martinis)

Make sure your vodka is frozen for a nice chilled Cosmo. Mix all the ingredients and shake your bootie until lemon has a chance to make some juice in the shaker, pour in a frozen martini glass and enjoy!

White Russian

2 ounces of Ketel One or Absolute Vodka

1 ounce of Kahlua

3 ounces of skimmed or 2% milk

This is a great drink to have after dinner while still enjoying your company. Just mix the above ingredients together and sip slowly because it takes like a delicious milk shake.

Six Figures Friendship Recipe

Must-Have Ingredients:

LOVE . . .then

Trust

Respect

Support

Great listening skills

A wonderful sense of humor

Patience

Understanding

Caring

An open mind, and . . .

More unconditional love

Mix all of these ingredients each time you get together with your friends and you can't miss.

The rewards will be yours and theirs.

CPSIA information can be obtained at www.ICGtesting.com
Printed in the USA
LVOW100205210113

316398LV00002B/68/P